# ABC of
# Medical Law

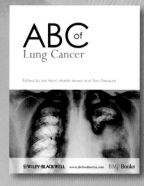

# ABC of
# Medical Law

## Lorraine Corfield
Senior Vascular Fellow, Guy's and St Thomas' NHS Trust, London, UK

## Ingrid Granne
Clinical Research Fellow and Specialist Registrar, Nuffield Department of Obstetrics and Gynaecology, University of Oxford, UK

## William Latimer-Sayer
Lawyer, Clinical Negligence and Personal Injury Specialist

WITH CONTRIBUTIONS FROM
## Ruth Wilkinson
Centre for Social Ethics and Policy, Institute for Science, Ethics and Innovation, School of Law, University of Manchester, UK

**WILEY-BLACKWELL**
A John Wiley & Sons, Ltd., Publication

**BMJ | Books**

*Library of Congress Cataloging-in-Publication Data*

Corfield, Lorraine, 1971–
  ABC of medical law / Lorraine Corfield, Ingrid Granne, William Latimer-Sayer.
    p. ; cm.
  Includes bibliographical references and index.
  ISBN 978-1-4051-7628-6   1. Medical laws and legislation – Great Britain. I. Granne, Ingrid. II. Latimer-Sayer,
William. III. Title.
  [DNLM: 1. Legislation, Medical – Great Britain. 2. Malpractice – legislation &
jurisprudence – Great Britain. 3. Patient Rights – legislation & jurisprudence – Great Britain.
4. Research – legislation & jurisprudence – Great Britain. W 32.5 FA1 C797a 2009]
  KD3395.C67 2009
  344.4104′1 – dc22

                                                                                  2008052024

A catalogue record for this book is available from the British Library.

Set in 9.25/12 Minion by Laserwords Private Limited, Chennai, India.
Printed and bound in Singapore by Markono Print Media Pte Ltd
1 2009

# Contents

# Preface

Medical law touches upon all areas of health care. However, it often appears complex and remote from daily practice. This book aims to alter this perception: it provides a concise outline of the basics of medical law and, by using commonly encountered situations and real legal cases, its practical application. The law is constantly evolving, and medical practitioners need to be aware of the latest legal developments: for example, national guidelines incorporated into legal decisions and new statutes, such as the Mental Capacity Act 2005 (explained in this book), are clearly relevant to all practitioners. A clinical practice consistent with modern medical law is essential for all professionals and should be adopted as a daily routine rather than only considered if and when a complaint is made. Ignorance of the law provides no defence and practitioners have a professional duty to keep up to date with the current law as it affects them and their patients.

This book is aimed at all qualified and student healthcare practitioners, both in hospital and primary care settings. It is also relevant to those involved in running a healthcare service, such as hospital, departmental and practice managers. It is not an exhaustive text but seeks to provide a concise overview of the most salient aspects of law as it affects day-to-day medical practice, and in particular, the main areas of concern that a junior doctor is likely to encounter during his or her training. Although the law cited is correct at the time of the book going to print, all practitioners must be aware that the law frequently changes as new cases are decided and new statutes passed. If any doubt exists in any particular situation, legal advice should be sought.

We hope that the *ABC of Medical Law* will increase awareness of the current legal position but also inspire interest in and decrease trepidation of the law in the world of clinical practice.

# CHAPTER 1

# Introduction to the Legal System

*Ingrid Granne*[1] *and Lorraine Corfield*[2]

[1]Clinical Research Fellow and Specialist Registrar, Nuffield Department of Obstetrics and Gynaecology, University of Oxford, UK
[2]Senior Vascular Fellow, Guy's and St Thomas' NHS Trust, London, UK

## OVERVIEW

- The law in the United Kingdom consists of statute and common law.
- Medical law mainly involves civil rather than criminal cases.
- Most medico-legal cases are heard in the High Court but appeals can be made to the Court of Appeal and finally to the House of Lords if the case is considered to be of sufficient public interest.
- Cases that relate to the Human Rights Act may ultimately be appealed to the European Court of Human Rights (ECHR).

You must keep up to date with, and adhere to, the laws and codes of practice relevant to your work.
— GMC: *Good Medical Practice* (2006)

The practice of medicine must take place within the boundaries of the law. The law regulates many aspects of medicine and therefore healthcare professionals must be familiar with the law in the area in which they work. Many healthcare professionals during the course of their career will be required to give written or verbal evidence to a court, either because of involvement with cases brought before the coroner or increasingly frequently because of medical litigation. It is therefore essential to have a clear understanding of how the legal system works.

## Case law

Historically, the legal system within the United Kingdom was based largely on law developed by judges over time. Judges would consider specific cases with reference to how similar points of law had been decided in past cases and apply the law as they found it to the case brought before them. This is known as a 'common law' system, in contrast to law that is made by parliament (which is known as 'statute law').

Each part of the United Kingdom developed its own forms of common law, with Scotland being especially distinct from the other

*ABC of Medical Law*. By Lorraine Corfield, Ingrid Granne
and William Latimer-Sayer. Published 2009 by Blackwell Publishing,
ISBN 978-1-4501-7628-6

countries of the United Kingdom. This book deals mainly with the law in England and Wales but does highlight some instances where Scottish law differs. On occasion, when there is no relevant domestic case law, judges may look to cases from other countries. Usually these cases are from countries within the Commonwealth (such as Canada and Australia) where the law has been developed in a way similar to that in the United Kingdom.

## The concept of precedent

A pronouncement by a judge regarding a particular issue of law may affect the way future cases are decided. Decisions made by one court in relation to a particular issue can become binding on judges considering the same issue at a later date. This is known as precedent. Such precedents are only set by judges in senior courts (the High Court, the Court of Appeal and the House of Lords) and apply to the courts equal to or below them. Precedent has a very important role in common law. It attempts to ensure consistency in the law while also allowing for the law to develop over time. To understand how precedent works, familiarity with two legal concepts, *ratio decidendi* and *obiter dictum*, is needed.

No two legal cases are identical and thus it may appear difficult to understand how a statement of law made in one case can apply to another. The courts do look back to find cases where the facts of the case are similar, but more importantly they try to see if the reasoning in a case can be applied to a new set of facts. Thus, judges must follow the *ratio decidendi* (meaning 'the reason for deciding') of an earlier judgement if it was made by a higher or equal court.

In many court cases, a judge may make comments that do not relate directly to the case. For example, the judge may state how they would have decided a case if the facts had been different, or make general comments regarding the area of law under scrutiny. This is known as *obiter dictum* (meaning 'a thing said by the way'). These pronouncements are not binding on judges, but may be used when considering similar issues in the future (Box 1.1).

Box 1.1 **Ratio and obiter explained: the case of *Briody v St Helen's and Knowsley AHA* (2001)**

A woman lost her baby during childbirth and required a hysterectomy as a result of negligent treatment. She desperately wanted a family and was considering surrogacy. The Court of Appeal ruled that it was not appropriate for her to recover the costs of surrogacy (the *ratio decidendi*). Thus this decision binds any Court of Appeal or lower court case of a similar nature.

The judge also stated that in her view the cost of other treatments such as *in vitro* fertilization (IVF) using donor eggs would also not be recoverable as damages in a negligence claim. This statement was *obiter dictum* and is not binding but may be used by lawyers to support their arguments should such a case arise.

## Reporting and documenting case law

As previously stated, many areas of law in the United Kingdom are dominated by case law (Figure 1.1). Thus, it is essential that there is a logical and methodical documentation of important and relevant cases. Since decisions regarding cases will depend on the *ratio* of cases decided previously, both lawyers and judges need access to accurate reports of previous judgements. In this book many real cases are used as examples to illustrate points of law and standard legal citations are used to describe them. For the healthcare professional interested in the basics of medical law, it is sufficient to know that a citation includes the two parties involved (for example, *Airedale NHS Trust v Bland*) and the year in which the case was heard. Other letters may indicate which level of court heard the case (for example, 'CA' refers to the Court of Appeal) or

in which publication the case was reported (for example, 'All ER' refers to the All England Law Reports).

In some cases such as those involving children, or cases regarding sensitive medical decisions, the names of the parties are not disclosed. In these cases, the initials and a very brief description of the main issue are used: for example, *Re B (child) (termination of pregnancy)* (1991).

A case citation is usually given in this format:

*Sidaway v Board of Governors of the Bethlem Royal Hospital* [1985] 1 ALL ER 643 (HL).

This shows the names of the two parties involved (Sidaway and the Board of Governors of the Bethlem Royal Hospital), the year the case was heard (1985), the place the case was published (the All England Reports) and that it was heard by the House of Lords (HL).

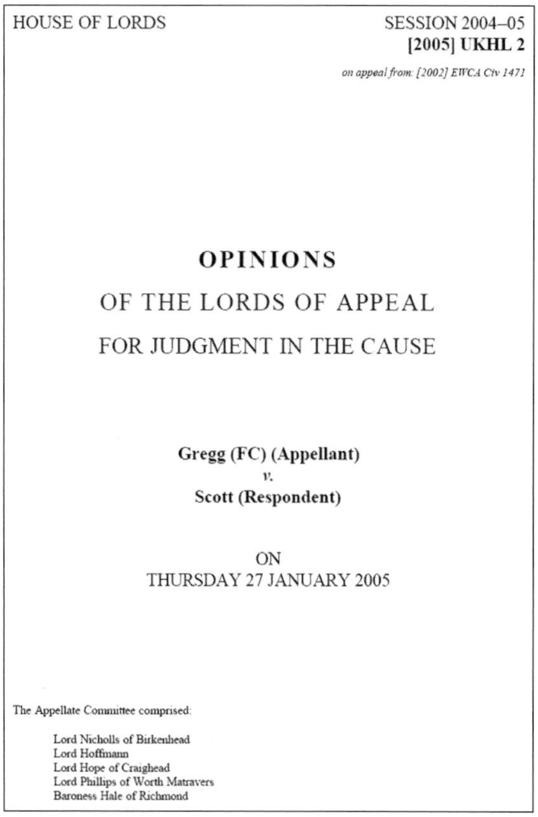

## Statute law

Since the seventeenth century, new laws and law reforms have increasingly been brought about through Acts of Parliament, usually inspired by policies of the government of the day. These Acts of Parliament will often become law in all parts of the United Kingdom. However, sometimes an Act may become law in part of the United Kingdom such as England and Wales, but not in Scotland.

Statutes are documents that contain laws made by Acts of Parliament (Figure 1.2). Statute law is known as primary legislation. Each statute relates to a particular issue. For example, the Abortion Act 1967 deals specifically with the way in which abortion is regulated, and the Mental Capacity Act 2005 defines capacity and how those who lack capacity should be treated with regard to their healthcare (among other things).

New legislation decided by parliament overrides previous case law. Case law cannot overrule or change statutes. The relationship between case law and statute law reflects the acceptance that parliament is the supreme law-making authority in the land. This is known as the doctrine of parliamentary sovereignty. For example, the decision as to whether a person is competent to accept or refuse treatment has in the past been determined by case law. The Mental Capacity Act 2005 now expressly defines competence in the eyes of the law and this 'overrules' previous case law concerning capacity. However, statutes may be updated or amended. The 1990 Human Fertilisation and Embryology Act amended the 1967 Abortion Act to decrease the legal limit for most abortions from 28 to 24 weeks. In addition to statutes, healthcare professionals must be aware of relevant accompanying legislation and guidelines (Box 1.2).

There are still many areas of medical law where no legislation exists and therefore common law prevails. For example, there are no statutes relating to the ability of children to consent to treatment. The well-known law concerning minors receiving contraception without parental knowledge is still derived from the decision made in the 1986 case of *Gillick v West Norfolk and Wisbech Area Health Authority*.

HOUSE OF LORDS                              SESSION 2004–05
                                                  **[2005] UKHL 2**

                                      *on appeal from: [2002] EWCA Civ 1471*

### OPINIONS

OF THE LORDS OF APPEAL

FOR JUDGMENT IN THE CAUSE

Gregg (FC) (Appellant)
*v.*
Scott (Respondent)

ON
THURSDAY 27 JANUARY 2005

The Appellate Committee comprised:

Lord Nicholls of Birkenhead
Lord Hoffmann
Lord Hope of Craighead
Lord Phillips of Worth Matravers
Baroness Hale of Richmond

**Figure 1.1** Gregg v Scott (2005); an example of case law.

# Human Fertilisation and Embryology Act 1990

CHAPTER 37

LONDON: HMSO

**Figure 1.2** The Human Fertilisation and Embryology Act. 1990. An example of statute law.

rules. For example, the Code of Practice for the Mental Capacity Act 2005 provides guidance and information on how the Act will work on a day-to-day basis for anyone who works with or cares for people who lack capacity. Healthcare professionals are legally required to follow the Code when acting or making decisions on behalf of people who lack capacity. Codes of Practice are more readable than the original statute and are therefore often a good place to start when wishing to understand a particular Act of Parliament.

### Medical Guidelines and the Law

Although guidelines (such as those published by the GMC and the Royal Colleges) and local protocols are not part of the law, it is clear that where no clear law exists with regard to a particular issue the courts will take into consideration such guidelines. Healthcare professionals also have a good practice obligation to abide by guidelines.

## The difference between civil and criminal law

The law consists of civil and criminal law. Criminal law deals with offences that the society has decided to 'outlaw' as crimes, such as

---

Box 1.2 **Accompanying legislation and guidelines**

**Statutory Instruments**

Sometimes Acts of Parliament provide a way for parliament to delegate law-making powers to another body. The main type of delegated legislation is known as a Statutory Instrument (SI). Whereas Acts of Parliament are primary legislation, SIs are referred to as secondary legislation. Most SIs are not required to be laid before Parliament, and are therefore not subject to any Parliamentary scrutiny. This allows for frequent or rapid changes in the law when necessary.

SIs often consist of an order, regulations or rules. For example, rules pertaining to how the General Medical Council (GMC) deals with allegations of a doctor's fitness to practise are laid down in an SI known as the General Medical Council (Fitness to Practise) Rules Order of Council 2004. This SI was made under the powers conferred by The Medical Act 1983. SIs themselves can be amended: the aforementioned GMC SI was amended in May 2008 to change the standard of proof required in Fitness to Practise cases to that of civil proceedings (see following text).

**Codes of Practice**

Many Acts of Parliament have an accompanying Code of Practice. Codes of Practice are legal documents that guide individuals or officials in the interpretation of an Act of Parliament. However, Codes of Practice are more than just guidance: they are legally enforceable

**Figure 1.3** The Royal Courts of Justice, London.

murder, rape or theft. Civil law is largely concerned with areas of the law relating to the legal relationship between people or legal entities such as companies or government. Areas of law such as those that regulate contracts, employment, issues of negligence or libel are all civil law. Many offences may be criminal or civil, and the distinctions between the two types of law can be complex. For example, it is possible for medical negligence to be either criminal or civil. However, most medical law pertains to civil rather than criminal law.

The standard of proof in civil law is that of the balance of probabilities: it has to be shown that there is more than a 50% chance that a civil wrong had occurred. The standard of proof in criminal cases is more stringent: the jury must find the defendant guilty 'beyond reasonable doubt'.

## The court system

Many healthcare professionals' first encounter with the courts is either while giving statements to, or while attending an inquest in a coroner's court. The work of this type of court will be covered in detail in Chapter 11. The Court of Protection (Box 1.3) deals with cases relating to the Mental Capacity Act 2005 (see Chapter 2).

> Box 1.3 **The Court of Protection**
>
> The Court of Protection is a new court with a specific role to make decisions in relation to the property, affairs, healthcare and personal welfare of adults (and sometimes children) who lack capacity. The court was created by the Mental Capacity Act 2005. This Act is discussed in more detail in Chapter 2. The court has the same authority in relation to mental capacity matters as the High Court and therefore is able to set precedents.
>
> The Court of Protection has the power to:
>
> * decide whether a person has the capacity to make a particular decision for themselves
> * make declarations, decisions or orders on financial or welfare matters affecting people who lack capacity to make such decisions
> * appoint deputies to make decisions for people lacking capacity to make those decisions.

Most other medico-legal cases are heard initially in the High Court. The High Court sits at the Royal Courts of Justice in London (Figure 1.3), as well as at some major court centres around the

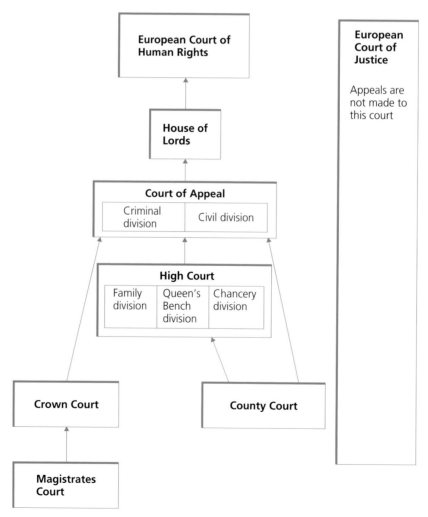

**Figure 1.4** The English court hierarchy.

country. There are three divisions within the High Court, each hearing specific types of cases. These are known as the Queen's Bench Division, the Chancery Division and the Family Division. Most negligence claims are brought in the Queen's Bench Division. However, life and death matters such as an application to withdraw life support are usually brought in the Family Division. A decision made by a court may be appealed, provided permission is granted to appeal by the initial trial judge or by the Court of Appeal. Appeals are made to the Court of Appeal, which also sits at the Royal Courts of Justice. Appeals are usually heard by three judges.

The highest court in the English legal system is the House of Lords. It has the final jurisdiction over both civil and criminal cases and deals solely with appeals. Only cases that are considered to be of public importance are heard by the House of Lords. Usually five 'law lords' consider each case, and the verdict is decided by a majority opinion. The House of Lords receives appeals from the courts in England, Wales and Northern Ireland, and civil cases from Scotland. The House of Lords will be replaced by The Supreme Court in October 2009.

For most legal cases, the House of Lords is the final point of appeal. However, in cases relating to Human Rights (such as the right to life and the right to privacy), claimants may be able to appeal to the European Court of Human Rights (ECHR).

The United Kingdom joined the European Community (now the European Union (EU)) in 1973. One consequence of this is the requirement to incorporate European legislation into UK law.

English law must be interpreted in a way that is consistent with European law. This includes not only the ECHR but also the European Court of Justice, which rules on matters of EU law. English courts must recognize the jurisdiction of the European courts (Figure 1.4).

## Further reading

Database of UK primary legislation at http://www.statutelaw.gov.uk/ [2008]

Guide to the judicial system at http://www.direct.gov.uk/en/CrimeJusticeAndTheLaw/Thejudicialsystem/DG_4003097 [2008]

Her Majesty's court system website provides information relating to the courts at http://www.hmcourts-service.gov.uk/index.htm [2008]

Holland J, Webb J. *Learning Legal Rules*, 5th edn. Oxford University Press, Oxford, 2003.

UK Acts of Parliament since 1996 are published by the Office of Public Sector Information at http://www.opsi.gov.uk/acts.htm [2008]

## General further medical law reading

Brazier M . *Medicine, Patients and the Law*, 4th edn. Penguin, London, 2007.

Machin V, Levington F, Dean P. *Medicolegal Pocket Book*. Churchill Livingstone, Singapore, 2003.

Marguand P. *Introduction to Medical Law*. Butterworth Heinemann, Oxford, 2000.

Mason JK and Laurie GT. *Law and Medical Ethics*, 7th edn., Oxford Universtity Press, Oxford, 2006.

# CHAPTER 2

# Consent in Adults

*Lorraine Corfield*[1] *and Ingrid Granne*[2]

[1]Senior Vascular Fellow, Guy's and St Thomas' NHS Trust, London, UK
[2]Clinical Research Fellow and Specialist Registrar, Nuffield Department of Obstetrics and Gynaecology, University of Oxford, UK

## OVERVIEW

- The principle of autonomy underlies the law regarding consent.
- Legally valid consent is competent, voluntary and informed.
- The Mental Capacity Act 2005 is central to treating incompetent adults.
- Decisions made under this Act must be in the best interests of the patient.

> For a relationship between doctor and patient to be effective, it should be a partnership based on openness, trust and good communication.
> – GMC: *Consent: patients and doctors making decisions together* (2008)

## Why is consent important?

The idea of patient autonomy is central to the provision of good medical care. It is a fundamental principle that every person's body is inviolate. The courts have repeatedly held that without valid consent or other legal authority, physical interference with another person's body is unlawful. Therefore, not only are there legal consequences for healthcare professionals who fail to obtain consent, but both the law and good practice also dictate that the practitioner should provide the relevant facts and alternatives to the patients who should then be allowed to decide the best treatment for themselves.

Furthermore, as a Court of Appeal judge stated in a case known as *Re W (a minor) (medical treatment)* (1993), 'The clinical purpose [of consent] stems from the fact that in many instances the cooperation of the patient and the patient's faith ... in the efficiency of the treatment is a major factor contributing to the treatment success'. This is perhaps most obvious where active patient participation is needed, such as dietary modification in diabetes or physiotherapy for back pain, but is also generally applicable.

*ABC of Medical Law.* By Lorraine Corfield, Ingrid Granne
and William Latimer-Sayer. Published 2009 by Blackwell Publishing,
ISBN 978-1-4501-7628-6

## The legal consequences of failure to obtain consent

Consent is required for everything that a healthcare professional does to a patient. Failure to obtain consent could lead to a charge of criminal assault (very rarely) or result in a civil claim for battery. Furthermore, failure to advise adequately in relation to risks associated with a particular treatment, while not necessarily amounting to an assault or battery, may amount to negligence (discussed in Chapters 5–7).

A charge of battery may arise whenever there is an intentional touching of a person without consent or other lawful justification. This could be anything from taking blood pressure to performing major surgery. It is important to be aware that the patient need not be harmed: if a healthcare professional touches, injects or operates on a mentally competent patient without valid consent the professional may still face a charge of battery even in the absence of any adverse consequences.

## What comprises legally valid consent?

The law makes it clear that consent must be:

- given by a competent person
- voluntary
- informed.

## Competence: The Mental Capacity Act 2005

The Mental Capacity Act 2005 (MCA) came into effect in 2007 and overrides any previous law on capacity (in law, capacity is synonymous with competence). It is relevant to any healthcare decision involving a patient who may lack capacity and generally applies to individuals aged 16 and above (Box 2.1).

Box 2.1 **Underlying principles of the MCA**

- A person must be assumed to have capacity unless it is established that he lacks capacity.
- A person is not to be treated as unable to make a decision unless all practicable steps to help the person have been taken without success.

- A person is not to be treated as unable to make a decision merely because he makes an unwise decision.
- An act done, or decision made, under this Act for, or on behalf of, a person who lacks capacity must be done, or made, in their best interests.
- Regard must be had to the person's rights and freedom of action. The decision must restrict these as little as possible.

## Assessment of capacity

The law presumes that a person has capacity until proven otherwise. However, healthcare professionals regularly treat people who may lack capacity and need to be able to assess this. Under the MCA, there are two main requirements before a person can be said to lack capacity.

Firstly, the person must have an impairment of, or disturbance in, the functioning of the mind or brain. This can either be permanent (such as severe learning difficulties) or temporary (such as drug or sepsis-induced confusion). However, the healthcare professional must always remember that a person can have such impairment but still be competent to make the decision in question.

Therefore, in addition to identifying such impairment, the professional must also demonstrate that the patient is unable to achieve at least one of the following:

(a) Understand the information relevant to the decision.
(b) Retain the information for long enough to make a decision.
(c) Use or weigh the information.
(d) Communicate the decision.

Information must be given to the patients in a manner that they can understand. For instance, a person who has learning difficulties may be able to understand what is proposed if the information is provided in an appropriate way. The MCA places emphasis on autonomy and if a person is able to make decisions with the benefit of assistance, then all available help should be given to allow that person to meet the four-stage test given earlier. A common example of this is someone whose first language is not English. Capacity may be in doubt if discussions are solely in English: the use of an interpreter will usually clarify the issue (Box 2.2).

---

Box 2.2 **How to help persons make their own decisions: requirements of the MCA Code of Practice**

- Use simple language.
- Keep information to that necessary for the decision.
- Consider the use of pictures and non-verbal communication.
- Enlist the help of others (relatives, support workers, speech and language therapists).
- Choose the time of day when the person's understanding is at its best.
- Choose a location where the person is at ease.

---

This may well mean arranging a meeting with the patient, relatives and support workers in a calm area away from the ward or at the patient's own residence. Considerable time may need to be taken to try various methods of communicating the information needed. The only exception to this would be in a true emergency where there is insufficient time for such an approach to be taken.

A person is permitted to make an irrational or unwise decision without being deemed incompetent. Medically inadvisable decisions, such as a person with a change in bowel habit refusing a colonoscopy, are not necessarily incompetent decisions. A common example is a Jehovah's Witness refusing blood products: this is a decision that a competent adult patient is entitled to make even if considered irrational by the treating health professional (for further discussion see Chapters 3 and 4).

## How to treat the incompetent patient: acting in best interests

If incapacity is established, the MCA then states that the healthcare professional must act in the best interests of the patient. These interests are not specified in the Act but under existing case law these are more than simply medical: they include psychological, emotional and social interests. For example, it may be in the best medical interests for a woman to have regular breast cancer screening with mammography but if she cannot understand the procedure and why it is needed, it may be very traumatic for her. The benefit of the test may be outweighed by the psychological damage if it is performed.

In assessing best interests under the MCA, healthcare professionals must consider:

- how to include the patient in the decision
- the incompetent person's past and present wishes, feelings and beliefs
- the views of the family and any carers of the patient
- each decision individually: a patient may be competent for one decision, such as a blood test, but incompetent to consent to complex surgery.

Although the final decision as to best interests will rest with the professional, who should record the reasoning behind the decision (Box 2.3), the following persons should be consulted and their opinions taken into account:

- Anybody who has been named by the person to be consulted.
- Any non-paid carer of the person.
- Close relatives, friends or others interested in the welfare of the person.

---

Box 2.3 **Documentation of decisions made under the MCA**

Practitioners should record their assessment of capacity when capacity is in doubt (this will sometimes involve documenting that a patient has capacity when this may not be immediately obvious) and the process of working out what is in that person's best interests. The Code of Practice states that the following should be recorded and kept on file in the assessment of best interests:

- How the decision about best interests was reached
- What the reasons for reaching the decision were

---

- Who was consulted
- What particular factors were taken into account.

The MCA protects practitioners from liability if they have acted in good faith. Contemporaneous documentation provides good support for the practitioner, should the need arise.

## Proxy decision-making

Although the views of the family and carers must be taken into account, they cannot consent on behalf of the patient. However, for the first time in English law the MCA allows a competent adult to appoint another adult to deal with medical decisions should they become incompetent. This appointed adult is called a donee of lasting power of attorney and may be a family member, carer or any other adult. This adult can provide consent for the patient. If the decision involves withdrawing or withholding life-sustaining treatment, the documentation appointing the donee must state this. A donee of lasting power of attorney differs from an enduring power of attorney in that the latter cannot make any medical decisions on another's behalf (but should usually be consulted as an individual interested in the patient's welfare).

In cases where there is no donee, a court may choose to appoint a deputy, invariably a family member or someone who knows the patient well, to make decisions for the incompetent person. A healthcare professional cannot overrule the decision of a donee or deputy. However, donees and deputies must act in the best interests of the patient and if the healthcare team feel that they have not done so then they should discuss this with the donee or deputy. Failing this, legal advice will be needed and as a last resort an application may be made to court to attempt to overrule the donee or deputy's decision.

## Independent mental capacity advocates

If the patient lacks capacity and has no family or friends whom it would be appropriate to consult, then the healthcare professional generally makes the decision on the basis of the team's assessment of the patient's best interests. However, in certain circumstances, an Independent Mental Capacity Advocate (IMCA) must be instructed (unless emergency treatment is needed). An IMCA should be appointed when the patient lacks capacity for the decision and there is no one else appropriate to consult in the following situations:

Providing, withholding or stopping serious medical treatment (treatment with serious consequences, where the risks and benefits are finely balanced or where the choice of treatment is finely balanced). This includes electroconvulsive therapy, chemotherapy, cancer surgery, major surgery, amputation, therapeutic sterilization and treatment resulting in permanent loss of sight or hearing

Decisions about whether to admit the person into hospital or move to another hospital for 28 days or longer

Decisions about admitting the person to longer-term accommodation such as a nursing or residential home, sheltered or ordinary housing or a hostel for more than 8 weeks

If the admission is an emergency or develops into a longer admission (greater than 28 days in hospital or 8 weeks in longer-term accomodation) than expected, an IMCA should be consulted as soon as possible (Box 2.4).

The IMCA must also be consulted in adult protection issues even if there is a relative or other individual to consult. Healthcare professionals should be aware of how to access an IMCA (Box 2.5).

---

**Box 2.4 The MCA in relation to rehabilitation and long-term care: an example**

A previously healthy 73-year-old man who lived alone was admitted for emergency care with a stroke. He lacked the capacity to decide about treatment. No relatives or friends were contactable, except for a nephew who was unwilling to be involved with decisions regarding his uncle's care. His initial care was on the stroke unit, was not considered serious treatment and was planned at less than 28 days. Therefore, for his initial treatment instructing an IMCA was not necessary and treatment decisions were taken by the healthcare team. Unfortunately, it shortly became clear that he would need longer-term (more than 8 weeks) placement in a nursing home. His capacity for this accommodation decision was assessed and all agreed that he was not competent to decide about placement. As there was no other adult to consult, an IMCA was instructed. The IMCA agreed with the healthcare team that long-term nursing home care was in the patient's best interests.

---

The IMCA cannot be involved in admission for or treatment of a mental illness under the Mental Health Act 1983 but should be instructed if the criteria mentioned earlier apply to a patient detained under the Mental Health Act who needs treatment or transfer for a physical condition. The IMCA is a specifically trained individual who collects information and forms an assessment as to what would be in the person's best interests. They have the right to access medical records. The healthcare professional remains the final decision-maker but must take the IMCA's report into account. The IMCA can challenge the decision-maker and insist on a second medical opinion. Communication between all involved will be central to making the best decision for the patient.

---

**Box 2.5 How to access an IMCA**

Arrangements will vary locally. The following should be able to provide details of how to instruct an IMCA in the region:

- Patient Advice and Liaison Service (PALS)
- Citizens' Advice Bureau
- Community Health Councils in Wales
- Department of Health via www.dh.gov.uk/imca
- The Hospital Trust's legal department.

---

## Decisions requiring court authorization

The court *must* be involved in certain situations:

• If the practitioner disagrees with the decision of a donee or court appointed deputy

- If there is a dispute between different healthcare professionals regarding capacity or best interests
- If there is a dispute between the practitioner and family.

and these differences cannot be resolved by any other means, such as arbitration.

A court order must also be sought for the following decisions where the patient is not competent:

- Non-therapeutic sterilization (such as hysterectomy to avoid pregnancy in a non-competent adult)
- Withholding or withdrawing artificial nutrition and hydration from a patient in a permanent vegetative state
- Organ and bone marrow donation
- Certain cases of termination of pregnancy.

### Restraint

As the incompetent person may not understand what is being done to him, restraint is sometimes necessary. However, certain conditions must be met for restraint to be legal:

- Restraint must be necessary to prevent harm to *the patient*.
- Restraint must be proportionate to any potential harm that would occur were the patient not to be restrained.

Thus, one cannot restrain a patient with dementia because they are disturbing others on the ward by shouting but could do so to stop them wandering around the ward if they are unsafe and at real risk of falling. The less restrictive option should be chosen: this is more likely to be putting the bed sides up than chemical sedation.

### Consent in emergencies

In an emergency, the defence of necessity allows a practitioner to treat a non-competent patient without consent. However, the healthcare professional must make a reasonable effort to fulfil the conditions of the MCA and must assess and act in the best interests of the patient. Therefore, a doctor may be reasonably expected to discuss the treatment plan with a relative who is present during an emergency but may not be expected to telephone other carers if time does not allow.

### Voluntary consent

Consent must be given freely for it to be valid. Coercion (often unintentional) may be by the practitioner himself or by friends and family. In practice, a competent patient who gives consent is rarely challenged and concerns about coercion are more relevant to refusal to consent (see Chapter 4).

### Informed consent

Doctors tend to use the term 'informed consent' quite liberally. However, the information legally required for valid consent (to avoid committing battery) only need be enough for the patient to understand the nature and purpose of the planned procedure.

This means that the healthcare professional must explain in broad terms what the procedure entails and why it is being carried

**Figure 2.1** When a medical student performs an examination, the nature and purpose of the examination must be made clear to the patient.

out. For valid consent, the professional does not need to discuss risks, benefits and alternatives in detail (but note that if they do not, they may be liable for charges of negligence: see Chapters 5–7). For example, to avoid a charge of battery (but not necessarily negligence), a doctor or nurse inserting a coil would have to explain that it is a device that is placed transvaginally into the uterus with the purpose of preventing pregnancy.

Care must also be taken in relation to the position of medical students. It is good practice for specific consent to always be obtained in relation to students performing procedures. This is particularly relevant in the case of a medical student performing an examination on a patient where the sole purpose of that examination is the education of the medical student (Figure 2.1). In this scenario the purpose of the procedure is different and specific consent must be obtained stating this purpose. This is well recognized for vaginal examination but should be equally practised for all other examinations such as fundoscopy and blood pressure measurement.

## Who should take consent?

Generally speaking, consent should be obtained (or at least confirmed) by the healthcare professional carrying out the procedure as it is that professional who will probably be liable for charges of battery if the consent is not valid. However, according to the Department of Health (DoH) and the General Medical Council (GMC), a healthcare professional can take consent if they are suitably trained and have the appropriate knowledge to seek consent for that procedure. However, the practitioner carrying out the procedure has overall responsibility for ensuring that consent is valid.

## Types of consent

In practice, consent is often verbal or clear from the patients' behaviour: they cooperate by rolling up a sleeve to allow their blood pressure to be taken. Provided the consent is valid (competent, voluntary and informed) such non-written consent is lawful. However, a signed consent form is certainly good and well-established

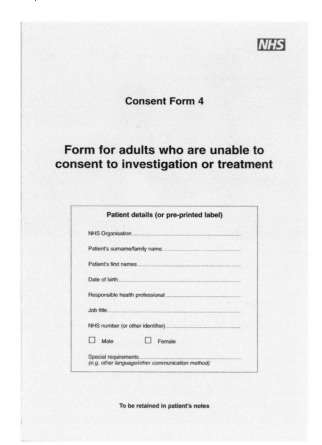

**Figure 2.2** Specific forms are often used for patients who are unable to consent to treatment.

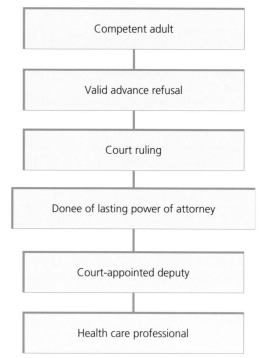

**Figure 2.3** Hierarchy of decision-making for adults.

practice for major interventions such as surgery, and would be of great importance should a legal case be brought as it provides a record of the consent process (including the associated risks that were explained).

The DoH produced four model consent forms in 1992. Trusts may have individual policies as to which form should be used and this should be followed but there is no current legal ruling as to the use of a particular consent form (Figure 2.2).

## Timing of consent

There is no specific law regarding when consent should be taken in relation to when a procedure is carried out. However, the practitioner must ensure that consent remains valid at the time of the procedure.

**Cases with key points: *Mohr v Williams* [1905] 104 NW 12 (Supp Ct Minn)**

***Background***: Consent had been taken for surgery to the right ear. However, while the patient was under anaesthetic, the surgeon found a more serious problem with the left ear, on which he operated with a good outcome, but without consent.

***Court Ruling***: The patient succeeded in a claim of battery against the surgeon.

***Key Points***: The *nature* of the operation for which consent was given was surgery on the right ear only, and the *purpose* was to improve the trouble she was having with her right ear, not to treat an incidental, non-emergency problem with her left ear, although that treatment probably benefited her in the long run. The treatment went beyond consent.

**Brushett v Cowan [1991] 2 Med LR 271 (Newfoundland, CA)**

***Background***: Consent had been taken for a muscle biopsy in the thigh, but during the operation an abnormal area of bone was found and biopsied.

***Court Ruling***: The charge of battery against the surgeon was not held up in this case.

***Key Points***: The *nature* of the operation was to biopsy a thigh abnormality and the *purpose* was to determine the cause of the problem for which the surgeon had been consulted. This operation had not gone beyond consent and no battery had taken place. Although these cases are not strictly binding as they are not English cases, such cases are relevant in English law (as discussed in Chapter 1).

## Further reading

General Medical Council. *Good Medical Practice*. 2006.
http://www.gmc-uk.org/guidance/good_medical_practice/index.asp
[2008]

General Medical Council. *0–18 Years: Guidance for all Doctors*. 2007.
www.gmc-uk.org/guidance/ethical_guidance/children_guidance/index.asp
[2008]

General Medical Council. *Consent: Patients and Doctors Making Decisions Together*. 2008.

IMCAs: www.dca.gov.uk/legal-policy/mental-capacity/mibooklets/booklet06.pdf [2008]

MCA Code of Practice: www.dca.gov.uk/legal-policy/mental-capacity/mca-cp.pdf [2008]

Mental Capacity Act 2005. www.dca.gov.uk/menincap/legis.htm [2008]

# CHAPTER 3

# Consent in Children

*Ingrid Granne*[1] *and Lorraine Corfield*[2]

[1] Clinical Research Fellow and Specialist Registrar, Nuffield Department of Obstetrics and Gynaecology, University of Oxford, UK
[2] Senior Vascular Fellow, Guy's and St Thomas' NHS Trust, London, UK

---

## OVERVIEW

- Sixteen and seventeen year olds are treated as adults for the purpose of consent.

- Children under 16 can consent if competent; otherwise parental consent is required.

- Consent on behalf of a child must always be in that child's best interests.

---

*Good Medical Practice* states that doctors must safeguard and protect the health and well-being of children and young people. Well-being includes treating children and young people as individuals and respecting their views, as well as considering their physical and emotional welfare.

— GMC: *0–18 years: guidance for all doctors* (2007)

Legally, a child is any person under the age of 18. However, the approach to consent differs between 16 and 17 year olds and those under 16. This chapter focuses on capacity to consent but as with adults, consent must also be voluntary and informed. Parents, overtly or otherwise, can affect the voluntariness of the consent and this should be considered if a child is consenting to a procedure.

## Consent in 16 and 17 year olds

A child who has reached 16 years of age can consent to any medical, surgical or dental treatment. This is clearly stated in the Family Law Reform Act 1969. Thus 16 and 17 year olds are generally assumed to be competent to consent in the same way as adults. If concerns about capacity to consent exist, these must be addressed as per the Mental Capacity Act 2005. If a child over 16 is not competent, a parent can provide consent in England, Wales and Northern Ireland. However, in Scotland, such children are treated legally in the same way as an adult lacking capacity.

Even a competent 16 or 17 year old cannot consent to blood or organ donation without the additional consent of someone with parental responsibility. No 16 or 17 year old can refuse life-saving treatment: this topic is covered in Chapter 4.

## Consent in children under 16

Unlike children aged 16 and 17, those under 16 are assumed to lack capacity. However, as all healthcare professionals will be aware, children vary in their understanding and some clearly have the capacity to consent. This was the issue brought before the courts in the well-known case of *Gillick v West Norfolk and Wisbech Area Health Authority* (1986). This tested the principle that a child under the age of 16 is not competent to consent to medical treatment, and therefore cannot be treated without the knowledge and agreement of a parent. The House of Lords ruled that children under 16 can consent if they are capable of understanding what is involved (often referred to as 'Gillick' competence or sometimes 'Fraser' competence after one of the judges in the case). Although this case was about a child seeking the oral contraceptive pill without parental knowledge, (Box 3.1) it applies to medical treatment in general.

As with adults, a young person may well have the capacity to consent to a relatively straightforward procedure or treatment while simultaneously lacking the capacity to consent to a complex procedure or to a treatment with serious risks. For example, a child with leukaemia may be able to consent to a course of antibiotics but may lack the capacity to consent to a bone marrow transplant.

The General Medical Council (GMC) is clear that doctors and other healthcare professionals must make themselves available to see a child or young person on his own if that is the wish of the child. The impression that attendance with a parent is necessary must be avoided.

---

Box 3.1 **Prescribing contraception to children under 16**

Prescribing contraception is legal without parental knowledge provided that:

- the child has capacity

- consent is voluntary (there may be pressure from partners or boyfriends)

- the child is encouraged to consult the parent(s)

---

*ABC of Medical Law.* By Lorraine Corfield, Ingrid Granne
and William Latimer-Sayer. Published 2009 by Blackwell Publishing,
ISBN 978-1-4501-7628-6

- the child is over 12 (intercourse with a child under 13 years is rape, even if seemingly consensual, and should be disclosed to the appropriate authority)
- the sexual activity is not abusive or seriously harmful (this should also be disclosed).

The GMC Guidance on providing contraception, abortion and sexually transmitted infection treatment and advice to children under 16 without parental knowledge states that this is acceptable provided that the child:

- understands the advice and its implications
- cannot be persuaded to discuss with or allow discussion with the parents
- is very likely to have sexual intercourse in any event

and that

- the child's physical or mental health is likely to be affected without the treatment
- it is in the child's best interests to have the treatment without parental knowledge.

## Who can consent for a child who lacks capacity?

In this situation, consent will usually be provided by a parent or person with parental responsibility (Box 3.2).

---

**Box 3.2 Adults with legal parental responsibility**

- Mothers
- Married fathers, even if there has been a subsequent divorce
- Unmarried fathers of children born after 1/12/2003 in England and Wales, 15/4/2002 in Northern Ireland and 4/5/2006 in Scotland, provided that the father's name is on the birth certificate
- Adoptive parents.

Other unmarried fathers, civil partners and step-parents can apply for parental responsibility.

If the child is in local authority care, the parents share responsibility with the local authority (which can restrict the parental responsibility).

Parental responsibility is lost if the child is given up for adoption.

---

Healthcare professionals may be faced with circumstances where the person who presents with a child is not a parent, but a teacher, school matron, neighbour, babysitter or other carer. In these circumstances, the law allows adults who do not have parental responsibility for children but who are caring for them to give consent to medical treatment (provided that they are safeguarding or promoting the child's welfare). However, a carer is only likely to need to give consent in the case of an emergency or if authorized

to do so by the parents (for example, for a child away at boarding school or on a school trip). Under normal circumstances, every effort must be made to contact a parent or a person with parental responsibility to obtain consent. In addition, in an emergency, medical professionals may use the defence of necessity to justify treating a child without parental consent. The court can also provide consent for a child if a case is brought and must be consulted if the child is a ward of court (this means that the court is the guardian of the child and all decisions about that child's upbringing must be approved by the court).

A doctor can treat a child who lacks capacity without parental consent in the following circumstances:

- An emergency if a parent is not available in time
- Parental neglect
- Abandonment of the child
- Inability to find the parent.

If both parents refuse to consent but the doctor feels that treatment is in the child's best interests, that doctor must seek legal advice and it is likely that the case will need to be taken to court for a ruling. The European Court of Human Rights has made it very clear that when doctors want to treat an incompetent child in the face of parental refusal then legal advice must be taken early with appropriate recourse to the courts. It is not acceptable to wait until the situation becomes an emergency. Of course, if a true emergency arises the doctor must proceed in the best interests of the child, but a legal ruling should have been acquired before this eventuality if at all possible.

As always, anyone providing consent for a child must act in that child's best interests. These are not limited to best medical interests but include psychological, social, emotional and educational needs. It may be clinically best to repair an incidentally found hernia as soon as possible but in the child's overall interests to wait until a set of exams or a school term is over. Although the wishes and feelings of the child must also be considered and may carry more weight as the child gets older, these wishes are not necessarily determinative of the decision. The welfare of the child must be paramount (Box 3.3).

---

**Box 3.3 Assessing best interests for a child lacking capacity**

The following should be considered:

- The clinically indicated treatment options
- The views of the child
- The views of the parents and anyone else close to the child
- The cultural, religious and other beliefs of the child and family (but see Box 3.4)
- The views of other professionals, healthcare and otherwise, who have an interest in the welfare of the child
- The extent to which the treatment will restrict the child and his future options (generally the least restrictive option should be chosen).

Adapted from the GMC. *0–18 years: guidance for all doctors* (2007)

---

## Box 3.4 **Blood transfusion and religious objections**

Adult Jehovah's Witnesses can refuse blood products provided they are competent (see Chapter 4). However, several cases have shown that parents who are Jehovah's Witnesses cannot refuse blood or blood products for their children if these are potentially life saving. As this is so well recognized, most Jehovah's Witnesses will allow their children to be transfused. If, however, they refuse, unless it is a true emergency when doctors can transfuse without parental consent, legal advice must be sought. Jehovah's Witnesses also have access to Hospital Liaison Committees to advise patients and parents in such circumstances.

## Will the consent of one parent suffice?

Generally, the consent of one parent is legally sufficient. However, where major or controversial treatments are planned, the healthcare professional would be well advised to consult both parents and seek legal advice if there is a problem in contacting the second parent or if there is irreconcilable difference between the two.

Care is needed in cases of immunization, cosmetic surgery or ritual circumcision (but not circumcision for medical purposes such as phimosis). If one parent refuses to give consent, legal advice is necessary even if the other parent provides consent (Figure 3.1). Legal advice should be sought in cases of termination of pregnancy, organ and bone marrow donation and contraceptive sterilization.

## Case with key points: B (a child) (Welfare of Child: Immunisation) [2003] EWCA Civ 1148

*Background*: Two similar cases were considered by the courts together. Both concerned the immunization of a child to which the mother was opposed whereas the father felt strongly that his child should be immunized.

*Court Ruling*: Immunization was in the children's best interests and was recommended by the courts. The judges had regard to 'all relevant factors and not just the assessment of medical risks and benefits'. Although each mother would find the decision to immunize her child difficult, this would not significantly affect her

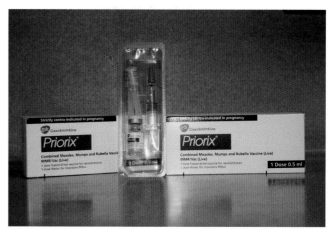

**Figure 3.1** Court advice must be sought if parents disagree about vaccinations for their children.

relationship with her child. The feelings of one of the children was taken into account (the other child was 4) and the judge found that she would accept the court's decision and agree to immunization. The judge stated that 'hotly contested issues of immunization' should be taken to court where parents disagree.

*Key Points*: Best interests are more than best medical interests. The child's opinion should be taken into account. Cases where immunization is felt to be in a child's best interests but one parent disagrees should be brought before the court.

## Further reading

British Medical Association. *Parental Responsibility. Guidance from the Ethics Department*. 2006. www.bma.org.uk/ap.nsf/Content/Parental [2008]

General Medical Council. *Good Medical Practice*. 2006. http://www.gmc-uk.org/guidance/good_medical_practice/index.asp [2008]

General Medical Council. *0–18 Years: Guidance for all Doctors*. 2007. www.gmc-uk.org/guidance/ethical_guidance/children_guidance/index.asp [2008]

# CHAPTER 4

# Refusal of Medical Treatment

*Lorraine Corfield[1] and Ingrid Granne[2]*

[1]Senior Vascular Fellow, Guy's and St Thomas' NHS Trust, London, UK
[2]Clinical Research Fellow and Specialist Registrar, Nuffield Department of Obstetrics and Gynaecology, University of Oxford, UK

## OVERVIEW

- A competent adult can refuse any treatment even if it is life saving.
- A valid advanced refusal of treatment is binding on healthcare professionals.
- Children under 18 cannot refuse life-saving treatment.

You must respect a patient's decision to refuse an investigation or treatment, even if you think their decision is wrong or irrational.
– GMC: *Consent: patients and doctors making decisions together* (2008)

## Refusal of treatment by adults

### When is a refusal valid?

A refusal for a medical procedure is valid if the same criteria as for valid consent are met (see Chapter 2). A valid refusal is:

- given by a competent adult
- voluntary
- informed.

The capacity and best interests of a patient lacking capacity should be assessed as per the Mental Capacity Act 2005 (see Chapter 2). However, when a patient who lacks capacity refuses treatment, the best interests of the patient must be assessed in the light of that refusal. For example, a brain-damaged adult who sustains a cut in the garden may refuse a tetanus injection due to an inability to understand that it is of benefit. The medical benefit must then be weighed against the potential harm of restraining the patient and giving the injection: perhaps a valuable healthcare professional–patient relationship would be damaged, leading the patient to refuse more important treatment in the future.

When treating a competent adult, it is unlawful to override a valid refusal, even if that refusal will result in serious harm to the patient

or in that person's death. This is encountered by many healthcare professionals in the case of refusal of blood transfusion on a religious basis. This refusal must be respected if valid (Figure 4.1). The law places such import on patient self-determination that a pregnant woman can refuse treatment, such as caesarean section, even if the treatment is necessary to prevent the death of or significant harm to the unborn child (irrespective of gestation or viability).

---

**Appendix to NHS Consent form 1 for a person refusing a blood transfusion e.g. Jehovah's Witness** (To be completed in addition to Consent Form 1)

I hereby expressly withhold my consent to and forbid the administration to me of a transfusion of allogeneic (another person's) whole blood or any of its four primary blood components, red cells, white cells, platelets and/or plasma.

I refuse to predonate any of my blood for storage and later reinfusion into me or anyone else. I refuse the use of any sample of my blood for cross matching.

I request and will accept alternative non-blood medical management to build up or conserve my own blood, to avoid or minimise blood loss, to replace lost circulatory volume, or to stop bleeding. I agree to the use of non blood volume expanders, and pharmaceuticals that control haemorrhage and / or stimulate the production of red blood cells.

I specifically request that the following elements of patient choice be respected:

Medical products (initial <u>one</u> of the three choices below)

_____ a) I refuse all fractions derived from any primary component of blood
_____ b) I accept all fractions derived from any primary component of blood
_____ c) I want to qualify (a) or (b) above and my instructions are as follows:

\ _____

Medical procedures: (initial one of the three choices below and see also the consent form's

Statement of patient).

_____ a) I refuse any medical or surgical intervention involving the autologous use of my blood during an operation or ongoing treatment

_____ b) I accept any medical or surgical intervention involving the autologous use of my blood during an operation or ongoing treatment

_____ c) I accept only the following medical or surgical interventions involving the autologous use of my blood

_____

- My decision to refuse blood and choose non-blood management MUST BE RESPECTED EVEN IF MY LIFE OR HEALTH IS THREATENED by my refusal

- I accordingly absolve the health professionals involved in my care, the hospital and every member of the medical staff concerned from all responsibility and from any liability to me, or to my estate, or to my dependents, in any way arising out of or connected with this, my refusal to consent to blood-related treatment as detailed in this appendix.

Date:..............................................

Signed:.................................................

Witnesses to patient's signature:.................................................................
(Medical Practitioner)

.....................................

**Figure 4.1** A blood products refusal form used by Jehovah's Witnesses.

---

*ABC of Medical Law.* By Lorraine Corfield, Ingrid Granne and William Latimer-Sayer. Published 2009 by Blackwell Publishing, ISBN 978-1-4501-7628-6

The main exceptions to this are as follows:

1 Some treatments for mental illness when detained under the Mental Health Act 1983
2 Under the Public Health (Control of Disease) Act 1984, a court can order that a person who may be suffering from a notifiable disease be examined and investigated (Box 4.1). A person with a notifiable disease can be removed to or detained in a hospital but treatment cannot be forced on that person.

---

Box 4.1 **Notifiable diseases (notifiable to the local authority)**

Acute encephalitis
Acute poliomyelitis
Anthrax
Cholera
Diphtheria
Dysentery and food poisoning
Leprosy (notifiable directly to the Health Protection Agency)
Leptospirosis
Malaria
Measles
Meningitis/meningococcal sepsis
Mumps
Ophthalmia neonatorum
Paratyphoid fever
Plague
Rabies
Relapsing fever
Rubella
Scarlet fever
Smallpox
TB
Tetanus
Typhoid
Typhus
Viral haemorrhagic fever
Viral hepatitis
Whooping cough
Yellow fever.

The legal duty is on the doctor to notify the authority if they suspect or know that a patient is suffering from one of the above.

---

## Advance refusals

Advance directives ('living wills') are becoming increasingly common. Since October 2007 these have been legally binding under the Mental Capacity Act 2005 and must be respected by healthcare professionals. An advance directive can only be made by a competent adult (18 years or older) and refers to medical treatment in the event that the person lacks capacity in the future to consent to proposed treatment. It only applies to refusing treatment: a person cannot make a legally binding request for future treatment. Advance refusals can be verbal but must be written if they refer to the refusal of life-sustaining treatment (Box 4.2).

---

Box 4.2 **Advance refusals**

An advance refusal of life-sustaining treatment must:

- be in writing
- be signed and witnessed
- state clearly that the decision applies even when life is at risk.

Basic care that cannot be refused by an advance directive includes:

- warmth
- shelter
- basic hygiene
- offer of food and water by mouth.

---

If faced with a possible advance refusal, the doctor must consider three points:

- Does an advance refusal exist?
- Is it valid?
- Is it applicable?

*Example 1*
A 65-year-old man has had a stroke and is unable to walk, communicate or care for himself. It is highly unlikely that he will improve. He develops a severe chest infection. His wife brings in a written, witnessed and signed statement that he made a few years ago (when clearly competent) to the effect that if he was unable to have an independent life, he would not want any active treatment, including antibiotics. The advance refusal clearly exists, it was valid when made (unless there is evidence of coercion) and it applies to the situation: he is unable to be independent. Therefore, it would be unlawful to treat him actively. He should not be given antibiotics for his chest infection.

*Example 2*
A 45-year-old man is brought to the emergency department after a massive paracetamol overdose. He is unconscious. The police show the emergency team his suicide note, which states in writing that he does not want any treatment if he is found alive and clearly states he wants to die. He has signed the note. This note is an advance refusal and obviously exists. It is applicable as he has been found alive and will die without treatment. The important question is its validity: his capacity at the time of writing the note is in real doubt and the note and signature was not witnessed. As this is an emergency, if the team have good reason to doubt the validity of the refusal, they can lawfully treat the patient.

*Example 3*
An elderly lady is staying with her daughter for a few weeks. Unfortunately she develops severe back pain, collapses and is unresponsive. The daughter tells the general practitioner (GP) that her mother has an abdominal aortic aneurysm and has a written, signed and witnessed statement regarding this in her own home

which is 60 miles away. This says that if the aneurysm ruptures she would not want to go to hospital or have any treatment but be allowed to die. The GP is convinced the aneurysm has ruptured but the daughter is adamant that an ambulance should not be called. This is a difficult situation but there would be grounds for treating the patient if this was felt to be in her best interests as the existence of the advance refusal is in doubt. As it is an emergency and if real doubt about the advance refusal exists, the GP can legally treat her and call an ambulance. Similarly the hospital can treat her but must take the opinion of her daughter into account. If a decision to treat is taken, every effort should be made to find the advance refusal but this should not delay treatment.

The applicability of an advance refusal can be particularly problematic. Advance directives should be as specific as possible but particularly as the person making the directive does not have to discuss the contents with a doctor or lawyer, the situations in which it is applicable can be unclear. For example, a patient may have a written refusal of cardiopulmonary resuscitation if this will result in brain damage. However, it is usually impossible to predict such outcomes, so the directive may well be inapplicable if further discussion has not been possible before the arrest.

A doctor will be protected in law if the existence, validity (Box 4.3) or applicability of an advance refusal is in question despite reasonable efforts to ascertain these or if the medical situation is an emergency and treatment is required immediately. If time allows and doubt remains, legal advice should be sought from the Trust's legal department or an appropriate medical defence society. However, even in an emergency, a doctor cannot override a clearly valid and applicable advance refusal.

---

Box 4.3  **When is an advance refusal invalid?**

An advance refusal becomes invalid if:

- it has been withdrawn
- the patient has done something clearly contrary to the advance refusal
- the patient has *subsequently* conferred the power to make that decision to a donee of lasting power of attorney.

---

## Refusal of treatment by children

In contrast to its position on agreement of minors to treatment, English law is clear that those under 18 cannot refuse treatment that is potentially life saving or will prevent serious harm, provided such treatment is in their overall best interests. Force can be used to allow treatment if this too is in the child's best interests. A parent (or person with parental responsibility) can override the refusal of a child, whether competent or not, in these circumstances. The exception to this is major surgery or a major procedure (such as heart transplantation) where the competent child refuses but the parents consent. If time allows, the case should be taken to court.

There may be occasions where both parents and the child refuse treatment despite repeated discussion and information. In these circumstances a court order must be sought unless it is a true emergency when the healthcare professional is justified in acting in the best interests of the child. For example, a GP called to a child with a meningococcal rash can lawfully give a dose of antibiotics against the wishes of both parents and the child, provided the GP takes their refusal into account when assessing best interests and it is a true emergency.

This is not to say that a competent child can never refuse treatment. If the treatment is not for a serious condition (such as a large benign naevus) it should not be forced upon the child even with parental consent. In any case, it would be difficult to argue that treatment (in this case surgery) was in the child's overall best interests if the child refuses.

Although children who refuse life-saving treatment are generally found by the courts to lack capacity (see case with key points), several judgements have found that a court could overrule the refusal of a competent child in matters of life and death or serious harm, particularly if the child is made a ward of court. The particular concerns surrounding feeding children with anorexia have been considered at length by the courts: the legal position is summarized in Box 4.4.

---

Box 4.4  **Children with anorexia and force-feeding**

- If the child is not competent to consent and refuses feeding then it is lawful to force-feed the child.
- A child detained under the Mental Health Act 1983 (MHA) can be force-fed.
- The courts have ruled that a competent child who refuses feeding can be held and treated in a specialist centre without sectioning the child under the MHA.
- Reasonable force can be used to both keep the child in the specialist centre and to provide treatment.

---

**Case with key point: *Re E (a minor)* [1990] 9 BMLR 1**

***Background***: E was a 15-year-old practising Jehovah's Witness who suffered from leukaemia. He required blood transfusions as part of a life-saving chemotherapy protocol. He refused the transfusions. The local authority made E a ward of court.

***Court Ruling***: The court authorized the transfusion on the basis that E had no realization of the full implications that lay before him as to the process of dying although the judges accepted he knew he was likely to die without the transfusions.

***Key Point***: The court is unlikely to find a child capable of understanding what it means to face death and thus in effect does not allow any child to refuse life-saving treatment unless it can be shown that the treatment is not in the child's best interests.

---

## Further reading

Lewis P. Feeding anorexic patients who refuse food. *Medical Law Review* (1999); 7(1): 2–37.

Mental Capacity Act 2005. www.dca.gov.uk/menincap/legis.htm [2008]

MCA Code of Practice. www.dca.gov.uk/legal-policy/mental-capacity/mca-cp.pdf [2008]

# CHAPTER 5

# Negligence: The Duty of Care

*Ingrid Granne*[1] *and Lorraine Corfield*[2]

[1]Clinical Research Fellow and Specialist Registrar, Nuffield Department of Obstetrics and Gynaecology, University of Oxford, UK
[2]Senior Vascular Fellow, Guy's and St Thomas' NHS Trust, London, UK

## OVERVIEW

- There are three components to a claim of negligence: the existence of a duty of care, breach of that duty and causation.

- Every healthcare professional has a duty of care to their patients.

- The Trust is usually vicariously liable for the actions of its employees.

- Healthcare institutions have a separate duty to have safe systems for patient care in place.

---

If a person holds himself out as possessing special skills and knowledge, and he is consulted . . . by or on behalf of a patient, he owes a duty to the patient to use due caution in undertaking the treatment . . . he owes a duty to use diligence, care, knowledge, skill and caution in administering the treatment.

– Lord Hewart CJ. *R v Bateman* (1925)

---

Most healthcare professionals fulfil their duties diligently and take great care when treating patients. The suggestion that care is substandard, let alone negligent, is very distressing to those professionals involved. However, patients rightly expect competent medical care and if they are harmed as a result of a lack of this good care, the law entitles them to appropriate recompense. This is the basis of claims in negligence. The majority of negligence claims are civil but occasionally criminal negligence may occur (Boxes 5.1 and 5.2).

Negligence is an extremely complex area but one of growing concern to healthcare professionals and organisations (Box 5.3). It is broken down legally into three strands:

- The existence of a duty of care
- Breach of that duty
- Causation (harm as a result of that breach of duty).

For the claim of negligence to be successful, all of these three strands must be proven. Each will be covered individually in this and the following two chapters. However, the discussion in this book has been limited to the basics of negligence: whether or not there has been medical negligence in a particular case is heavily dependent upon the specific circumstances, and if in doubt, specific legal advice should be sought.

---

### Box 5.1 **Criminal negligence**

Criminal negligence occurs where such disregard for the life and safety of others is shown that the breach of duty should be characterized as gross negligence and a crime. This includes gross negligence (involuntary) manslaughter. This charge may be made if a healthcare professional causes death as a result of some blameworthy act on their part without actually intending to cause death or serious injury. For example, in 2003 a haematology registrar was convicted of manslaughter after instructing his senior house officer (SHO) to inject an intravenous chemotherapy agent into the spine despite the SHO querying the instructions twice (*R v Mulhem* (2003)).

Eleven charges of manslaughter were brought against doctors between 2000 and 2005. Although the number of doctors charged with manslaughter appears to be rising, the overall conviction rate remains low at about 30%.

---

### Box 5.2 **The Corporate Manslaughter and Homicide Act 2007**

This allows for the prosecution of hospitals, GP practices and private clinics for deaths due to negligence that are deemed to be manslaughter. This will usually be a consideration only in cases of serious systems failure.

---

### Box 5.3 **Negligence claims: The facts and figures**

- The NHS Litigation Authority received 5426 claims between 2006 and 2007 and paid out £579.3 million in damages and legal costs
- Approximately 40% of claims are dropped
- Approximately 40% are settled out of court
- Fewer than 50 cases per year are taken to court.

---

This chapter concentrates on the first strand of negligence: the existence of a duty of care. Both individual healthcare professionals

---

*ABC of Medical Law.* By Lorraine Corfield, Ingrid Granne
and William Latimer-Sayer.  Published 2009 by Blackwell Publishing,
ISBN 978-1-4501-7628-6

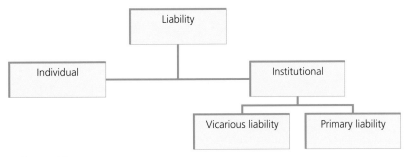

**Figure 5.1** Types of liability in negligence claims.

and healthcare institutions have a duty of care to their patients and may be liable for negligence if this duty is breached (Figure 5.1).

## Individual liability

### Doctors and the duty of care

Although the following two paragraphs are centred on the duty of care of a doctor, the same principles apply to all healthcare professionals. A nurse has a duty of care to all those admitted to the part of the ward or department to which that nurse is allocated. Physiotherapists, dieticians and other professionals owe a duty of care to those they assess and treat.

### Hospital doctors

It is generally clear when a hospital doctor owes a patient a duty of care: the patient will be under the care of an admitting team or the Emergency Department Consultant and juniors. Certainly a duty of care exists once a doctor has seen a patient. A doctor also undertakes a duty of care once he has given telephone or other advice. For example, an on-call medical registrar who gives advice after looking at an electrocardiogram (ECG) undertakes a duty of care (to provide non-negligent advice) even if the registrar does not subsequently see the patient. Similarly, a surgical registrar who is telephoned by an emergency doctor about a minor rectal bleed and who advises that the patient can be discharged with outpatient follow-up has a legal duty of care to that patient.

### General Practitioners

The undertaking of a duty of care is more complex for general practitioners (GPs) as they have a list of patients under their care who will not all be actively seeking advice. However, a GP does owe a general duty of care to those on their list, which is usually considered to become indisputable when a patient on the list seeks a consultation. In addition, GPs have a legal duty to seek and offer consultations to all newly registered patients within 28 days and to all those over 75 years of age on an annual basis. They also have a legal duty to see any individual who has not seen a doctor for 3 years if that patient requests a review.

### Private treatment

The duty owed to a private patient by a doctor providing private treatment is based on contract. This will have express terms, such as what treatment is to be provided and by whom. Beyond these express terms, the courts are clear that in this setting the private doctor has a duty to use reasonable care and skill but no duty to guarantee a particular outcome unless this has been part of the contract.

## Healthcare professionals and 'Good Samaritan' acts

Any healthcare professional who goes to the aid of an ill or injured person when they are not employed to do so undertakes a Good Samaritan act.

### The legal position

With the exception of GPs and midwives, there is no legal obligation on the healthcare professional to act as a Good Samaritan (for example, providing medical attention to someone who collapses in the street).

GPs, however, are obliged to treat an emergency or accident victim of whom they are aware in their practice area. This is irrespective of whether they are on or off duty provided that they are available and capable of providing care. The same obligation exists in the area of any primary care trust (PCT) on whose medical list the GP is included, provided the GP agrees to provide that treatment. Outside of these areas, the GP, like other doctors, has no legal obligation to assist in an emergency. The community midwives are in a similar position. Even if they are off duty they are likely to have a contractual legal duty to provide midwifery assistance in any obstetric emergency in the area in which they work.

### The General Medical Council

> In an emergency, wherever it arises, you must offer assistance, taking account of your own safety, your competence, and the availability of other options for care.
>
> – GMC: *Good Medical Practice* (2006)

Although there is no legal obligation for doctors other than GPs to stop and offer assistance in an emergency, failing to do so or to ignore a call of 'is there a doctor in the house?' is a violation of General Medical Council (GMC) guidelines and may amount to professional misconduct.

Therefore, in practice, doctors registered with the GMC should offer assistance in an emergency if it is safe to do so. It is exceptionally unusual for doctors to be sued for negligence when acting as a

Good Samaritan. There are strong public policy grounds against such claims succeeding because this would discourage doctors from helping people in need.

## The Nursing and Midwifery Council

The Nursing and Midwifery Council (NMC) clearly states in its guidelines that in an emergency setting, in or outside of work, nurses and midwives have a professional duty to provide care.

## Institutional liability

National Health Service (NHS) healthcare institutions also have a duty of care to patients. This consists of a primary duty of care to patients (see following text) and vicarious liability (liability for the negligence of the institution's employees). For the institution to be vicariously liable for the negligence of one of its employees, that employee must have been acting in the course of their employment when the negligence occurred. For example, an appendicectomy carried out by a theatre scrub nurse is unlikely to be seen as being within the course of her employment. If a negligence claim is brought, then her employer will probably not be vicariously liable. However, the employer may still be liable under its primary duty of care for allowing an unqualified member of staff to perform an appendicectomy and failing to carry out proper checks to ensure that such procedures were only undertaken by appropriately trained members of staff.

The law relating to private hospitals and clinics is less clear. Whether or not a primary duty of care is owed to the patient will depend on the particular facts of the case. In some instances there may be a contract with the hospital or clinic (or company responsible for running the hospital or clinic) to provide particular services, and a primary duty of care will be owed to the patient. In other instances it might be argued that the private hospital or clinic merely agrees to arrange introductions to competent health professionals (who are working on a self-employed basis) and the duty of care is owed directly by the individual treating clinicians.

When carrying out any private work it is important for health professionals to check their insurance position. A clinician acting on a private basis may or may not be covered by the hospital or clinic's indemnity. Confirmation should be sought as to whether or not individual insurance is required to cover the work being performed.

## NHS Trusts: Hospital employees
### Vicarious liability

The relevant NHS Trust will often (but not always; See box 5.4) be vicariously liable for any negligence of its employees provided that the negligence occurred during the course of their employment. Apart from the staff clearly employed by the Trust (most healthcare professionals are directly contracted to the Trust), NHS indemnity will cover the following:

- GPs working as clinical assistants for the NHS
- Locums (internal or external) doing the work of a doctor or other healthcare professional who would normally be covered by vicarious liability

- Students under the supervision of an NHS employee
- Junior NHS staff involved in the care of private patients in NHS hospitals if normally providing this care would be part of their NHS contract.

---

Box 5.4 **Personal Liability**

Doctors and other healthcare professionals remain personally liable for the following:

- Private practice
- Criminal acts
- Good Samaritan acts
- Acts that lead to disciplinary (GMC) proceedings
- Reports for insurance companies (unless undertaken on behalf of the NHS)
- Some negligence claims when working for the NHS (NHS indemnity should not be relied on).

Some of these may be covered by professional indemnity from a defence society: this is recommended for all practising clinicians.

---

### Primary liability

This duty of care consists of a duty on the hospital to ensure that safe systems and a safe healthcare environment are in place. This includes providing reasonable care, healthcare professionals of sufficient skill and experience, supervision for employees and adequate communication systems, facilities and equipment.

## General Practitioners
### Vicarious liability

GPs will only be covered by vicarious liability if they are employed by the Primary Care Trust (PCT) or NHS Trust. A GP practice will be vicariously liable for the negligence of any of its employees (including receptionists, nurses and doctors). Vicarious liability for district nurses, health visitors and community midwives will be provided by their employer (the Health Authority, NHS Trust or PCT).

### Primary liability

PCTs have a primary duty of care to ensure that the doctors they place on their lists are competent. GP practices have a primary duty to ensure that they take due care when appointing staff and to have safe systems in place (such as a system to ensure that urgent results are reviewed and acted on).

---

**Case with key points: *Bull v Devon AHA* [1993] 4 Med LR 117**

***Background***: A woman in labour with twins was taken to a two-site hospital. A suitable doctor was not available on the site to which she was taken. A delay in communication between sites resulted in delayed arrival of appropriate medical care and the second twin was brain-damaged as a result.

***Court ruling***: The hospitals had a duty to provide adequate staff, services and equipment for the provision of maternity services. The hospitals were in breach of their primary duty of care.

***Key points***: Hospitals and GP surgeries must have safe systems in place to ensure good patient care. If they do not, then they will be in breach of their primary duty and may be liable for any systems failure resulting in harm.

## Further reading

Ferner RE, McDowell SE. Doctors charged with manslaughter in the course of medical practice. *Journal of the Royal Society of Medicine* 2006; 99: 309–314.

Holbrook J. The criminalisation of fatal medical mistakes. *BMJ* 2003; 327: 1118–1119.

National Health Service Litigation Authority at www.nhsla.com [2008]

# CHAPTER 6

# Negligence: The Legal Standard of Care

*Ingrid Granne*[1] *and Lorraine Corfield*[2]

[1]Clinical Research Fellow and Specialist Registrar, Nuffield Department of Obstetrics and Gynaecology, University of Oxford, UK
[2]Senior Vascular Fellow, Guy's and St Thomas' NHS Trust, London, UK

---

## OVERVIEW

- The legal standard of care is the Bolam test.
- The standard of care is the same for all the healthcare professionals, whatever their level of experience.
- Clinical guidelines are becoming increasingly important in setting legal standards of care.
- Informing patients about their care (including divulging risks) is also judged by the Bolam test.

---

Legal proceedings should be treated as a last resort, to be used only when other means of resolving a dispute are inappropriate or have failed.

– *The Woolf Report* (1996)

---

Patients rightly expect a certain standard of care from healthcare professionals. Ascertaining this standard of care is a difficult issue, particularly as care inevitably varies between healthcare institutions and healthcare professionals. However, the courts have had to decide how this standard of care is established to allow those harmed by the medical profession to have a claim in negligence and receive compensation as appropriate. Not all errors are negligent and many negligence claims involve cases where no 'mistake' as such has been made. The key distinction is whether the care was substandard: in legal terms, whether the professional's duty of care had been breached.

## The legal test for standard of care: The 'Bolam Test'

This became the legal test for the standard of care required of doctors (and subsequently other healthcare professionals) following the case of *Bolam v Friern Hospital Management Committee* (1957) in which a claim of negligence was made against a doctor who administered electroconvulsive therapy without a relaxant or

restraint. The patient suffered a fractured hip as a result. The claim failed but the judge stated the following (now commonly known as the 'Bolam Test'):

A doctor is not guilty of negligence if he has acted in accordance with a practice accepted as proper by a responsible body of medical men skilled in that particular art.

The law has since clarified that simply providing a body of 'medical men' is not adequate. The body of medical opinion must be reasonable, respectable, responsible and logical (from the ruling in the *Bolitho* case: see 'case with key points' in Chapter 7 for details). It is a point of some controversy as to whether the *Bolitho* case has changed the Bolam test or merely emphasized its original meaning. However, in clinical practice and henceforth in this book, the 'Bolam Test' refers to the Bolam Test as interpreted after *Bolitho* (see Box 6.1). For example, a practice simply followed out of habit or convenience can be in itself a negligent practice, and thus, following such a practice may be no defence in a claim of negligence. Therefore general practitioners (GPs) or hospital doctors who use a familiar antibiotic to treat a chest infection rather than that recommended according to local antimicrobial policy may be open to a negligence claim, even if their colleagues would use the same antibiotic.

---

### Box 6.1 Bolam and Bolitho

Before the *Bolitho* ruling, the concern was that the Bolam Test could be interpreted as accepting any body of medical opinion rather than a 'responsible body'. Thus a healthcare professional facing a charge of negligence could produce a group of professionals who would have treated the patient in the same way and use this as a defence, irrespective of whether the treatment was acceptable.

Furthermore, this meant that medical practice set its own standards and these were not open to real review by the legal system.

However, the House of Lords in *Bolitho* effectively addressed the first concern by stating that the opinion had to be reasonable, respectable, responsible and logical. This may merely be a restatement of the Bolam Test, which dictated that the medical opinion must be 'responsible'. However, it served as a clear reminder of this and allowed judges to review medical evidence in this light. A judge can now find that medical evidence is not reasonable or responsible if it

---

*ABC of Medical Law.* By Lorraine Corfield, Ingrid Granne
and William Latimer-Sayer. Published 2009 by Blackwell Publishing,
ISBN 978-1-4501-7628-6

does not withstand logical analysis. But, as the court stated, 'it will very seldom be right for a judge to reach the conclusion that views genuinely held by a competent medical expert are unreasonable'.

The House of Lords in *Bolitho* also found that in negligence cases the judge 'will need to be satisfied that ... the experts have directed their minds to the question of comparative risks and benefits'.

Healthcare professionals cannot assume that because other professionals have the same practice as theirs they will be immune from a successful negligence charge.

## Healthcare professionals in training

The patient has a legal right to a certain standard of care, irrespective of the level of experience of the person providing that care. A healthcare professional who lacks experience or who is in training (such as a newly qualified doctor or nurse) must reach the standard of care of a reasonably competent and experienced professional. Lack of experience is no defence to a charge of negligence.

This has been tested in several cases, the best known being that of *Wilsher v Essex Area HA* (see Box 6.2). In his judgement, Lord Glidewell stated that 'the law requires the trainee ... to be judged by the same standard as his more experienced colleagues'. Junior clinical staff should not panic: the junior doctor who inserted the line incorrectly had discharged his duty of care by seeking senior help. However, professionals who undertake work beyond their competence, are open to a negligence claim should harm occur, particularly if they are not supervised (the exception being a true emergency; see below).

---

### Box 6.2 **Wilsher v Essex Area HA (1986)**

A very premature baby was admitted to a neonatal unit. Unfortunately a junior doctor placed an arterial line in a vein rather than artery and both this doctor and the senior registrar failed to spot the mistake on the post-procedure X-ray. As a result, unnecessary excess oxygen was administered to the baby. The baby developed retrolental fibrodysplasia, one cause of which is the administration of high-dose oxygen, and subsequently developed near-total blindness. A case of negligence was brought. Although breach of duty was established, on the facts of the case the claimant could not show that the excess oxygen delivery was the probable cause of the blindness as there were other possible causes of retrolental dysplasia, and therefore the claim for negligence was lost.

---

Senior doctors, NHS Trusts and GP practices must also ensure that juniors are adequately supervized: if they are not and mistakes occur, the senior doctor, trust or GP practice may be guilty of negligence.

Providing treatment in a true emergency is likely to be seen differently by the law: the standard of care is that which can be reasonably expected in the circumstances. For example, junior surgical trainees may be the most appropriate available persons to insert a life-saving chest drain during a trauma call even if they have not performed the procedure before. Should they cause further

**Figure 6.1** Courts are likely to take note of guidelines when the standard of care is in question.

damage, provided they had taken reasonable care, a court would be less likely to find them negligent than if they performed a similar procedure electively.

## The standard of care and clinical guidelines

The courts seem to be placing increasing import on available guidelines (such as The National Institute of Clinical Excellence (NICE) and General Medical Council (GMC) guidance) and may well use such guidelines when considering cases involving the standard of care (Figure 6.1). Healthcare professionals are, of course, legally permitted to deviate from any guideline in their practice when treating individual patients, provided the treatment has a logical basis. Professionals should carefully record why they have departed from clinical guidelines and ensure that the departure is reasonable and would stand up to scrutiny in court. Currently NICE guidance states that all patients should be commenced on aspirin after a myocardial infarction. If doctors do not adhere to this guideline (perhaps because of ongoing gastritis despite the use of a proton-pump inhibitor to suppress acid production) they should record the reasons for this. Doctors wishing to undertake innovative treatment not yet supported by national guidelines or a reasonable body of medical evidence are advised to go ahead only with full informed consent of the patient, with the support of the Trust and legal advice if appropriate.

## Keeping up to date

Healthcare professionals have a legal duty to keep up to date. The legal standard is that doctors should be aware of changes by

"The New Stop TB Strategy and the Global Plan, with the important new developments outlined in this issue, present an ideal opportunity to turn the tide against tuberculosis."

**Figure 6.2** Healthcare professionals should keep up to date by reading relevant journals.

reference to major textbooks and leading journals (Figure 6.2). The GMC, in *Good Medical Practice* (2006), states 'You must keep your knowledge and skills up to date throughout your working life. You should be familiar with relevant guidelines and developments that affect your work. You should regularly take part in educational activities that maintain and further develop your competence and performance' (Box 6.3).

---

Box 6.3 **Relevant guidelines**

Relevant guidelines with which the healthcare professional should keep up to date include the following:

- Department of Health
- GMC or relevant professional body
- Royal College guidelines
- Local and national protocols.

The GMC states that prescribing doctors must be familiar with the following:

- The British National Formulary (BNF)
- The BNF for children
- NICE guidelines (in England and Wales)
- The All-Wales Medicines Strategy Group (in Wales)
- The Department of Health, Social Services and Public Safety Guidelines (in Northern Ireland)
- The Scottish Medicines Consortium and NHS Quality Improvement Scotland (in Scotland).

---

Hospital trusts, primary care trusts (PCTs) and GP practices must also ensure that the people they employ have the opportunity to keep up to date. Healthcare professionals also have a responsibility to keep up to date with, and adhere to, the law relevant to their work such as the Mental Capacity Act 2005. Most statute law has an accompanying (and more readable) code of practice that explains how the law should be implemented. These codes may change over time and all professionals are expected to keep up to date with any relevant changes.

## The duty to give patients information

> In modern law medical paternalism no longer rules and a patient has a prima facie right to be informed by a surgeon of a small, but well established, risk of serious injury
>
> – Lord Steyn, *Chester v Afshar* (2004)

Chapter 2 has already covered the legal requirements in terms of information for consent to a treatment or a procedure to be legally valid: the patient needs to understand what is proposed and why.

Over and above this, the doctor (or other healthcare professional) has a duty to provide the patient with information about the risks of any treatment or procedure. If this information falls below a certain standard, and if harm occurs, the doctor may be liable for a claim in negligence. This standard is the same as that for any standard of care (indeed the duty to inform is not a separate legal duty but part of the general duty of care and thus subject to the same legal standard: namely that of the Bolam Test).

### What risks should be disclosed?

There is some case law governing what risks should be discussed with the patient although this is not as clear-cut as many healthcare professionals may believe. Several judges have made statements as to what risks should be disclosed, and opinions differ. Overall, a doctor's duty to inform is measured by what a reasonable body of medical opinion would logically regard as appropriate. However, healthcare professionals must note that there is legal precedent for a duty to inform of a substantial risk of serious adverse consequences and risks that may be particularly relevant to the patient. Therefore, GPs may not routinely warn a patient that the drug they have just prescribed can very rarely cause a permanent tremor. However, should that patient have a job where good hand control is vital (such as a portrait painter) then not to warn of this remote risk may well be seen as negligent should the permanent tremor occur.

The GMC agrees that patients should be aware of serious or frequently occurring risks. The guidelines suggest that amount of information given to each patient will vary depending on risks, complexity of treatment and the patient's wishes. They advise that doctors must do their best to find out about patient's individual needs and priorities but must not make assumptions about what patients would choose to know.

The law has provided no particular percentage level at which a risk should be disclosed. Frequently occurring risks (such as bleeding with warfarin) should be discussed with the patient. It can be difficult to know where to draw the line with less frequent risks. However, there is some case law from which the level of risk can perhaps be derived. The recent case of *Chester v Afshar* (see Chapter 7) provides some authority that a risk level of 1 to 2% for a serious side effect or complication should be disclosed. However, if a risk is particularly serious or relevant it is likely to be appropriate to discuss smaller risks. Risk discussion is generally not at the discretion of the healthcare professional (Box 6.4).

## The duty to answer questions

The law is clear: it is the duty of the healthcare professional to answer questions truthfully. This is an absolute duty and is not governed by the Bolam principle. Therefore, a healthcare professional cannot withhold the truth when asked, even on the basis that other professionals would reasonably have done the same.

## The duty to inform when mistakes occur

> If a patient under your care has suffered harm or distress, you must act immediately to put matters right, if that is possible. You should offer an apology and explain fully and promptly to the patient what has happened, and the likely short-term and long-term effects.
> – GMC: *Good Medical Practice* (2006)

If the mistake creates a need for further treatment for which consent is required, then it will be necessary to give details of the mistake so that the subsequent treatment can legally be undertaken. If an excessive dose of medication is given accidentally with the result that regular blood pressure measurements and intravenous access are required, the patient should be told that this is due to the error as the patient's consent may otherwise be invalid (due to lack of information and understanding as to why the monitoring is needed).

Aside from this, no case law covers the duty to tell patients if mistakes occur. This is not to say that a case could not be brought if a professional did not admit a mistake that impacted upon the patient's life. There are also ethical reasons for being honest with patients and the GMC guidelines state that doctors should be honest and act with integrity.

---

Box 6.4 **Therapeutic privilege**

The concept of therapeutic privilege is that a doctor can withhold certain information from a patient if the doctor deems it to be in the patient's best interests. This is a paternalistic practice and is not generally condoned by English law, which has an autonomy-based approach.

There may be cases when the healthcare professional genuinely decides that withholding information from the patient regarding a

---

risk is the correct course of action: this should only be considered where there is a chance of real harm. Even so, the healthcare professional is taking the risk of being charged with negligence. Very few legal cases apply the principle of therapeutic privilege, one of which is the Australian case of *Battersby v Tottman* in which a negligence case was brought against a psychiatrist who prescribed a high-dose antipsychotic without warning the patient of the risk of permanent eye damage. The judges found that it was reasonable for the doctor to have exercised therapeutic privilege. If he had disclosed the risk to the patient there was a real chance that the patient would have developed hysterical blindness and was therefore at real risk of harm from the disclosure. The psychiatrist was not found to be negligent.

The doctor may or may not have been found to be negligent in England. The GMC provides very limited support for exercising therapeutic privilege. The guidelines advise that information necessary for decision-making should not be withheld unless the doctor judges that disclosure of some relevant information would cause the patient serious harm. This does not include the patient becoming upset or deciding to refuse treatment. If time allows and the professional plans to withhold such information, legal advice would be a sensible precaution.

---

**Case with key points: *Marriott v West Midlands HA* [1999] Lloyd's Rep Med 23**

**Background**: A GP was called out to a patient who had been admitted to hospital overnight for observation several days previously after a head injury sustained falling downstairs. He complained of ongoing headaches and lethargy but neurological examination was normal. The GP prescribed painkillers and did not refer the patient back to hospital. The patient collapsed four days later with a large extradural haematoma. Despite evacuation of the haematoma he remained severely disabled.

**Court ruling**: The trial judge held that although there may have been only a small risk of a major problem, referral and computerized tomography (CT) scanning were readily available and the consequences of failing to arrange these were severe. The GP was held to have been negligent.

**Key points**: Even if there were a body of medical opinion supporting the GP's treatment, the judge found that it would not have been reasonable, thus applying the *Bolitho* case to the Bolam principle. The Court of Appeal agreed that a judge is entitled to reject expert opinion if it is not reasonable.

## Further reading

Current NICE guidelines at www.nice.org.uk [2008]
Department of Health guidelines at www.dh.gov.uk [2008]
General Medical Council guidelines at www.gmc-uk.org [2008]

# CHAPTER 7

# Negligence: Causation

*Ingrid Granne*[1] *and Lorraine Corfield*[2]

[1] Clinical Research Fellow and Specialist Registrar, Nuffield Department of Obstetrics and Gynaecology, University of Oxford, UK
[2] Senior Vascular Fellow, Guy's and St Thomas' NHS Trust, London, UK

---

**OVERVIEW**

- In most cases, harm has to be physical or psychiatric (rather than psychological) for damages to be awarded.

- The basic test for causation is the 'but for test'.

- For a successful claim, it has to be shown that the negligence was more likely than not (a greater than 50% chance) to have caused the harm.

---

Under our law as it is at present ... a claimant will only succeed if, on balance of probability the negligence is the cause of the injury. If there is a possibility, but not a probability, that the negligence caused the injury, the claimant will recover nothing in respect of the breach of duty.

– Lord Phillips, *Gregg v Scott* (2005)

---

Negligence in the eyes of the law is a very specific term. Lay people and healthcare professionals often refer to what they consider to be poor treatment as being 'negligent'. However, for the purposes of a civil claim in negligence, showing that a healthcare professional failed to attain the requisite standard of care is not sufficient to establish an entitlement to compensation. In addition, legally recognizable harm to the patient must have occurred (see Box 7.1) and the claimant (the injured party) must prove on a balance of probability (that is, more than a 50% chance) that the substandard care resulted in that harm.

---

**Box 7.1  The three strands of negligence**

A duty of care must exist.

That duty must have been breached (a reasonable standard of care was not attained).

That breach of duty must have caused harm (causation).

---

Practitioners should be aware that claims can be brought several years after the event occurred (Box 7.2).

---

*ABC of Medical Law*. By Lorraine Corfield, Ingrid Granne
and William Latimer-Sayer.  Published 2009 by Blackwell Publishing,
ISBN 978-1-4501-7628-6

---

Box 7.2  **Timing of claims**

There is a limitation of three years from the time of injury, or the time at which the claimant was aware that the injury was possibly caused by negligence, during which a claim can be brought. There are exceptions to this such as the following:

- The three years for children bringing a claim themselves runs from their eighteenth birthday, not from the time of injury.

- If a patient lacks capacity, the three years run from when capacity is regained.

- The court has the power to extend the three-year limit.

This is important for all healthcare professionals: a claim can be brought many years after the incident. Accurate, contemporary and comprehensive note-keeping is therefore essential for any claim to be defended.

---

## What does English law accept as harm?

To date, case law has been clear that harm must either be physical or psychiatric (injury resulting from the development of, failure to improve or worsening of a recognized physical or psychiatric condition). Physical injury (such as a nerve injury caused by surgical error) is often easy to identify. However, damages (Box 7.3) will not be recovered for psychological symptoms: to date, no court has awarded damages in a clinical negligence setting for mere distress as a result of negligent medical care (and it is likely that the claimant will need to be diagnosed as suffering from a psychiatric disorder categorized under the *Diagnostic and Statistical Manual of Mental Disorders IV* (DSM-IV) or International Classification of Diseases (ICD)-10 for damages to be successfully claimed). Similarly, relatives (bystanders) who suffer distress at witnessing inadequate care of another will not be able to claim damages for that distress. If, however, those relatives are diagnosed as suffering from a recognizable psychiatric disorder such as an adjustment disorder or a pathological grief reaction, they may be able to recover damages subject to a number of conditions as follows:

- There must have been a shocking event (such as witnessing a loved one suffering from a fatal fit).
- There must be a close tie between the claimant and the victim of the substandard treatment.

- The claimant must have been in sight or hearing of the event or its immediate aftermath.

---

**Box 7.3 Damages**

If the court finds that clinical negligence has resulted in harm, it will award damages. These are divided into *general damages* for the actual harm that occurred (which are often modest) and *specific damages* that are usually much larger since they include compensation for loss of earnings and the cost of any necessary ongoing care. Negligence proceedings are civil (unless the charge is criminal negligence) and the healthcare professional is not at risk of a custodial sentence. Assuming the care was provided in the National Health Service (NHS) the health professional concerned will often be covered by indemnity from the relevant Trust. However, proceedings are sometimes brought against individual practitioners, particularly against general practitioners (GPs) and those in private practice. Personal indemnity is therefore essential.

---

## Causation

This is a very complex area of clinical negligence and the explanation here is limited to the basic test of causation as this is the test most relevant to clinical practice. This is known as the 'but for' test. The claimant must show that the harm would not have eventuated 'but for' the negligence. The standard of proof required is the balance of probabilities (in contrast to, for example, the standard of proof required in criminal cases, which is of guilt beyond reasonable doubt). Therefore, there has to be a greater than evens (more than 50%) chance that the harm occurred as a result of the negligence. Note that the onus is on the claimant to show causation, whereas in battery charges, the onus is on the defendant to show that there was valid consent.

The case of *Barnett v Chelsea and Kensington HMC* (1969) demonstrates that the negligence has to be shown to have caused the subsequent harm. Three men attended an Accident and Emergency Department with vomiting. When the casualty doctor was contacted he recommended that the men see their own doctors as he himself was unwell. The hospital had undertaken a duty of care to the men, who were suffering from arsenic poisoning. One of the men subsequently died and his widow brought a negligence claim. However, she was not able to show that on the balance of probabilities the negligence had caused her husband's death: he was very likely to have died even had he been admitted and treated. Therefore the claim failed.

## Loss of chance

Patients have made negligence claims when a delayed diagnosis has meant that they have missed out on the chance of curative treatment or the delayed diagnosis has made their prognosis substantially worse. The normal rules of negligence apply using the 'but for' test: the claim is likely to succeed if there is a more than 50% chance that the negligence caused the harm. For example, if a diagnosis of acute lymphocytic leukaemia is not made in a young child with subsequently incurable disease and the medical evidence is that the delayed diagnosis reduced the chance of cure from 80% to 20%, it could be argued that 'but for' the missed diagnosis the child was likely (on the balance of probabilities) to have been cured.

The courts have been asked to rule on several occasions where, on the balance of probabilities the harm would have occurred in any event. Therefore, the usual 'but for' test cannot apply in these cases, the chance of improvement or cure is less than 50% even with treatment. Not surprisingly, patients feel aggrieved if they have lost the chance of a cure due to a delayed diagnosis, however small that chance. Some have brought cases widely known as 'loss of chance' cases. To date, all such claims have been unsuccessful. These cases are best illustrated by the case of *Hotson v East Berkshire AHA* (1987) in which an epiphyseal femoral fracture was initially missed. Necrosis of the femoral head resulted. The claimant could not show that the necrosis would not have occurred 'but for' the delay in diagnosis as there was only a 25% chance that immediate diagnosis and surgery would have prevented the necrosis. The claim was made for damages based on the loss of chance of full recovery. The case was appealed to the House of Lords who ruled that damages cannot be recovered for a loss of chance of less than 50%. More recently, the House of Lords heard the case of *Gregg v Scott* (2005) in which a delay in a diagnosis of lymphoma resulted in a decreased likelihood of 10-year survival from 42 to 25%. As there was a less than 50% chance of Mr Gregg surviving for 10 years even had he been diagnosed appropriately, he could not claim damages on a 'but for' basis. Again, the House of Lords ruled that in this case, damages should not be awarded for loss of chance.

## Chester v Afshar (2004): an important case

This case is worthy of discussion at more length because it is seen as a landmark case in medical law. The claimant had back pain and consulted Mr Afshar. She consented to a discectomy. It was not disputed in the case that the discectomy carried a 1 to 2% risk of paralysis and that it was good medical practice to warn of this risk. A lower court had ruled that Mr Afshar had negligently failed to warn Miss Chester of this risk and this was accepted by the House of Lords. Miss Chester underwent the discectomy and unfortunately sustained a spinal injury. The surgery itself was not negligent: the issue before the House was whether Miss Chester could claim damages as she was negligently not informed of the risk of paralysis. Before this judgment, a claimant would have needed to show that they would not have proceeded with surgery had they known of the risk in order to satisfy the 'but for' test. In these cases, the surgery and therefore the risk would not have occurred if the claimant had been warned of the risk and had decided against the procedure. However, Miss Chester did not claim this but stated that she would have reflected on the risks further and possibly obtained a second opinion. Thus, she would have had the operation on a different day. The court took it as fact (rightly or wrongly) that the risk of paralysis is random, assuming the operation is performed non-negligently, and therefore if she had surgery on a different day, the chance of spinal injury remained 1 to 2%. Therefore she was highly unlikely to have been paralysed by surgery on a different day and the House of Lords found in favour of Miss Chester.

This case was important because:

- it placed great emphasis on the autonomy of the patient: the patient has a 'right to know'
- the judges were concerned about the infringement of the patient's right to know as well as the physical damage that ensued
- the duty to inform is most important in those who find the decision to consent difficult
- it reiterated that the standard for disclosure of risks remains the Bolam Test.

However, before health professionals become too worried about the possible ramifications of this decision it should be noted that there has been considerable criticism of this judgment. Unless the claimants can show that had they been properly informed, a further opinion would have been sought and surgery carried out on a different day (and possibly by a different surgeon), a claim is unlikely to succeed.

## Summary of medical negligence

1 For a claim of negligence to succeed, the claimant (injured party) must show that:
   - the defendant owed the claimant a duty of care
   - the defendant breached that duty
   - the breach of duty resulted in harm to the claimant.
2 A possible breach of duty by healthcare professionals is assessed by the Bolam Test, which states that:

> A doctor is not guilty of negligence if he has acted in accordance with a practice accepted as proper by a responsible body of medical men skilled in that particular art.

3 Subsequent case law has added that that body of opinion must also be respectable, logical and reasonable.
4 The resultant harm must be physical or psychiatric and the claimant must show that on the balance of probabilities the negligence caused the harm. The usual test for causation is the 'but for' test.
5 Information giving is also subject to negligence law: the information that should be imparted will be judged by the Bolam test.

In addition, there is case law stating that small but serious risks should be disclosed. Questions must be answered truthfully.

---

**Case with key points: *Bolitho v City & Hackney Health Authority* [1998] AC 232**

***Background***: A two-year-old boy was an inpatient with croup. He deteriorated twice on the ward and the doctor was called on both occasions, yet failed to attend. In between each episode, the child recovered quickly but subsequently arrested, developed brain damage and died.

***Court Ruling***: A breach of duty was admitted by the defendant. It was also accepted by the court that if the child had been intubated before the arrest, the brain damage could have been avoided. However, opinions differed as to whether it would have been appropriate to intubate the child. The doctor who was called and failed to attend stated that she would not have intubated the child. The case went to the House of Lords as the Court of Appeal found in favour of the defendant, based on the opinion of one medical expert who stated he would not have intubated. The question then arose as to whether judges were required to accept a medical opinion as providing an acceptable standard of care without further scrutiny. The House of Lords ruled that in order to be accepted, the body of medical opinion had to be logical, reasonable and respectable and must to have weighed up the risks and benefits of the treatment option. However, the judges also ruled that it would be rare for a court to be able to decide that a medical opinion did not meet these criteria. *Bolitho* was not found to be one of these rare cases and the appeal was dismissed, thus, the House of Lords ruled in favour of the defendant. The lack of attendance on the part of the doctor, although constituting substandard care, had not caused the harm as the child would not have been intubated even had the doctor attended and the failure to intubate would not have been negligent.

***Key Points***: This case demonstrates the need to prove causation as well as breach of duty. The effect of the judgment on the *Bolam* test has been widely discussed in academic law. Opinion is divided as to whether it merely supports the initial description of the test, essentially emphasizing the use of the word 'responsible' or whether it adds to the test, making it more stringent. Whether the test is referred to as the *Bolam* test or the *Bolam/Bolitho* test, it is now clear that legally a body of medical opinion must be able to stand up to scrutiny as to its reasonableness and logical basis.

# CHAPTER 8

# Confidentiality

*Lorraine Corfield[1] and Ingrid Granne[2]*

[1] Senior Vascular Fellow, Guy's and St Thomas' NHS Trust, London, UK
[2] Clinical Research Fellow and Specialist Registrar, Nuffield Department of Obstetrics and Gynaecology, University of Oxford, UK

---

**OVERVIEW**

- Healthcare professionals have a duty of confidentiality to their patients.
- Disclosure of confidential information is usually only lawful with consent.
- Breach of confidentiality without consent may be lawful in certain circumstances, such as to prevent a serious crime or for public health reasons.
- Competent children are owed the same duty of confidentiality as adults.
- Confidential information must be kept physically secure.

---

All that may come to my knowledge in the exercise of my profession or in daily commerce with men, which ought not to be spread abroad, I will keep secret and never reveal.

*– Hippocratic Oath*

---

## The duty of confidentiality

A duty of confidence arises when one person discloses information to another, such as patient to healthcare professional, in circumstances where it is reasonable to expect that the information will be held in confidence. The legal duty arises from common law, although it is now a statutory requirement under Article 8 (the right to respect for private and family life) of the Human Rights Act 1998. All healthcare professionals are bound by this duty of confidence. This extends to all employees of any healthcare body, including contractors, students and voluntary workers. Every National Health Service (NHS) organization should have written information about confidentiality readily available to patients.

## What is confidential information?

Any information pertaining to patients must be treated as confidential. Anonymized information (with name, address, post code

and any other identifiable information removed) is not confidential and may be used with relatively few constraints. However, it is important to be aware that even if all seemingly identifiable information is removed, the existence of a rare disease may still allow identification of the person involved.

## Disclosure of confidential information

Confidential information can generally only be disclosed with the express consent of the patient. However, it may also be legally disclosed to the appropriate third party in two circumstances:

- Where there is an overriding public interest
- Where there is a legal or statutory requirement.

### Disclosure with consent

As with all consent, that for disclosure must be competent, voluntary and informed (see Chapter 2). If the person is unable to consent to confidential information being passed on, and the healthcare professional believes the person to be a victim of neglect or abuse then the professional should disclose this to the appropriate authority if they feel that disclosure is in that person's best interests. In addition, it is occasionally permissible to disclose information without consent for the public good under the NHS Act 2006 (see Box 8.1).

---

Box 8.1 **Disclosure under NHS Act 2006 s 251**

This allows disclosure of patient-identifiable information when consent cannot be obtained in certain circumstances for the public good. The Patient Information Advisory Group (PIAG) must be consulted and they must decide that there is a significant potential benefit (for example, for research purposes) before disclosure can occur. This only applies in England and Wales. In Scotland and Ireland, the Caldicott Guardian (usually a senior healthcare professional in each health institution who is responsible for safeguarding the confidentiality of patient information) should be consulted.

It is under this section that it is possible to store patient-identifiable information on cancer registries without express consent.

---

### Disclosure in the public interest

This should be undertaken with consent if possible. However, if consent is withheld some confidential information can or must be

*ABC of Medical Law.* By Lorraine Corfield, Ingrid Granne
and William Latimer-Sayer. Published 2009 by Blackwell Publishing,
ISBN 978-1-4501-7628-6

divulged in certain circumstances. Whether there is sufficient public interest to justify disclosure should be judged by the healthcare professional (with senior and legal advice if needed). The public interest to disclose must outweigh both the public interest in maintaining confidentiality and the obligation of confidentiality to the individual. This generally includes preventing or detecting serious crime, abuse or serious harm to others. The definition of serious crime is unclear but is likely to include the offences listed in Box 8.2. However, theft, fraud and damage to property where loss is not substantial are unlikely to be included. The General Medical Council (GMC) advises reporting any gunshot wounds to the police (anonymously unless the patient provides consent or there is an overriding public interest). The patient must be informed that the disclosure is taking place unless a violent response is likely or if disclosure may allow the person to escape custody or destroy evidence. In addition, doctors have a duty to inform the driver and vehicle licensing agency of a patient's medical condition in certain circumstances (Box 8.3). Informing partners of those with a sexually transmitted infection is at the discretion of the medical practitioner concerned (Box 8.4).

Box 8.2 **Serious crimes (which are likely to allow disclosure of confidential information)**

Murder and manslaughter
Rape
Treason
Kidnapping
Child abuse or neglect
Serious harm to an individual
Crimes involving substantial financial gain or loss
Serious harm to the security of the state or public order
Road traffic accidents
Terrorism

Box 8.3 **Fitness to drive and disclosing information**

The Driver and Vehicle Licensing Agency (DVLA) has an extensive list of medical conditions (such as epilepsy or the presence of a large abdominal aortic aneurysm) that may affect the ability to drive.

If a patient has one of these conditions the patient must be encouraged to stop driving and inform the DVLA.

Should the patient refuse, the healthcare professional should inform the DVLA and tell the patient that they have done so.

Box 8.4 **Sexually transmitted infections: informing partners**

At present it is the decision of the medical practitioner as to whether at-risk partners of a person with HIV or another sexually transmitted infection should be informed in the absence of consent. If a decision is made to discuss this with the partner then the identification of the patient should be kept confidential wherever possible.

There is also a confidential reporting system for public health monitoring of sexually transmitted disease, including HIV. There is a similar confidential reporting system for fertility treatment information under the Human Fertilisation and Embryology Act 1990. In other circumstances the express consent of the patient is required.

## Legal requirements to disclose

A court, including the Coroner's Court, can order disclosure. Although healthcare professionals must comply with this, they can object if the requested information seems irrelevant. However, the final decision of the coroner or judge is binding.

There are also several statutory requirements for disclosure to the appropriate authority. These include

(a) The Abortion Act 1967 and Abortion Regulations 1991 to give notice of the termination to the Department of Health. In addition, if an offence has taken place contravening the Act, the Director of Public Prosecutions must be informed (Figure 8.1)
(b) The Public Health (Control of Disease) Act 1984 and Public Health (Infectious Diseases) Regulations 1988. For a list of notifiable diseases see Box 8.1
(c) The Police and Criminal Evidence Act 1984. The police can apply to a judge for access to confidential medical information or samples. However, in addition to this, remember that if healthcare professionals decide that disclosure is necessary in the public interest (see preceding text), they can legally disclose this information to the police
(d) The Terrorism Act 2000 provides a legal obligation on every individual to disclose any information regarding the funding of terrorist activities.

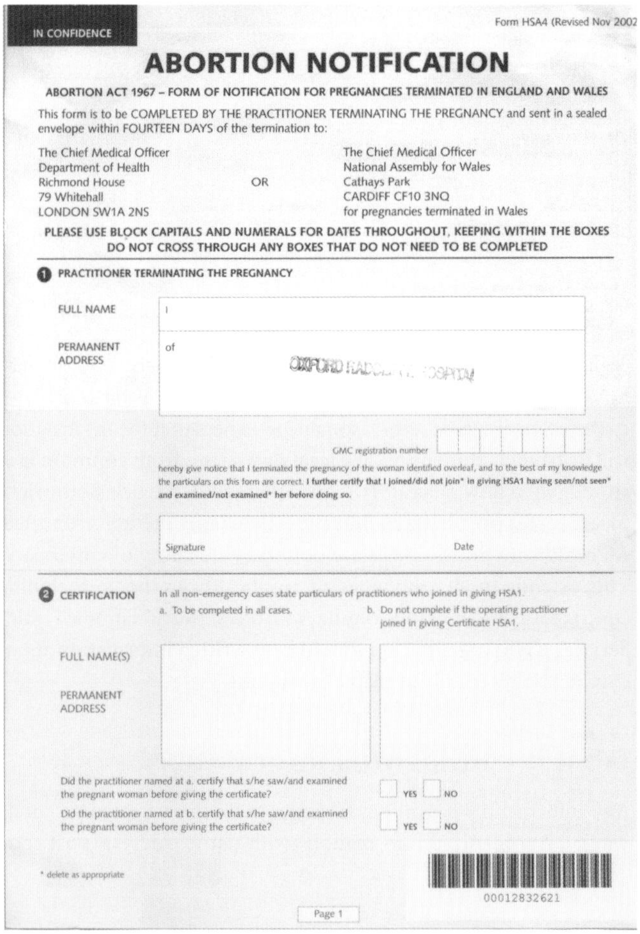
IN CONFIDENCE

Form HSA4 (Revised Nov 2002

**ABORTION NOTIFICATION**

ABORTION ACT 1967 – FORM OF NOTIFICATION FOR PREGNANCIES TERMINATED IN ENGLAND AND WALES

This form is to be COMPLETED BY THE PRACTITIONER TERMINATING THE PREGNANCY and sent in a sealed envelope within FOURTEEN DAYS of the termination to:

| | | |
|---|---|---|
| The Chief Medical Officer<br>Department of Health<br>Richmond House<br>79 Whitehall<br>LONDON SW1A 2NS | OR | The Chief Medical Officer<br>National Assembly for Wales<br>Cathays Park<br>CARDIFF CF10 3NQ<br>for pregnancies terminated in Wales |

**PLEASE USE BLOCK CAPITALS AND NUMERALS FOR DATES THROUGHOUT, KEEPING WITHIN THE BOXES**
**DO NOT CROSS THROUGH ANY BOXES THAT DO NOT NEED TO BE COMPLETED**

1 PRACTITIONER TERMINATING THE PREGNANCY

FULL NAME I

PERMANENT ADDRESS of

OXFORD

GMC registration number

hereby give notice that I terminated the pregnancy of the woman identified overleaf, and to the best of my knowledge the particulars on this form are correct. **I further certify that I joined/did not join* in giving HSA1 having seen/not seen* and examined/not examined* her before doing so.**

Signature Date

2 CERTIFICATION In all non-emergency cases state particulars of practitioners who joined in giving HSA1.

a. To be completed in all cases.

b. Do not complete if the operating practitioner joined in giving Certificate HSA1.

FULL NAME(S)

PERMANENT ADDRESS

Did the practitioner named at a. certify that s/he saw/and examined the pregnant woman before giving the certificate? YES NO

Did the practitioner named at b. certify that s/he saw/and examined the pregnant woman before giving the certificate? YES NO

* delete as appropriate

00012832621

Page 1

**Figure 8.1** There may be a legal duty to disclose information such as in cases of therapuetic abortion.

Doctors are no longer required to inform the Home Office if they believe a person is addicted to a controlled drug (such as diamorphine).

## Talking to relatives and friends

Information about a patient's condition should only be revealed to relatives or friends with the express consent of the patient. If the patient cannot consent, the healthcare professional will need to decide whether informing relatives and friends is in the best interests of the patient.

Giving information over the telephone is a particular concern and should generally be avoided. If there is no alternative, consent should be obtained where possible and precautions must be taken against people obtaining information by deception. The call should be returned before information is disclosed and details should be kept to a minimum. For example, if a relative calls and requests detailed information about a patient, in addition to gaining the consent of the patient, it may be prudent to ring back on a number given by the patient to ensure the caller is indeed the patient's relative.

## Discussions with healthcare professionals

The GMC states that if a patient has consented to treatment (such as referral or an X-ray) then express consent for a secretary to type a referral letter or for details to be put on an X-ray request form is not necessary. However, patients should be made aware that personal information about them will be shared within the healthcare team to enable them to object. This is particularly important when an outside agency (such as social services) is to be involved (unless there is an overriding public interest such as the safety of a child).

There may be professional reasons to discuss cases with colleagues for advice or to share experience and knowledge. Steps should be taken to ensure that others do not overhear and the patient should not be identified (this includes the discussion of cases in morbidity and mortality meetings).

Similarly, if a person rings claiming to be a healthcare professional involved in the care of the patient, if any doubt about the identity of that person exists, the call should be returned before information is given. Bogus callers will usually not provide a number for returning the call.

## Confidentiality and children

Young people are owed a duty of confidentiality. However, there is the additional matter of informing parents of their child's medical issues. As 16- or 17-year-olds are presumed to have the capacity to consent for themselves, they are entitled to the same duty of confidentiality as adults. The same applies to competent children under 16. Thus these individuals can legally demand that their parents are not informed of any consultation or its content. This includes prescriptions for contraception and consultations for teenage pregnancy (see Box 8.5). The doctors should encourage children to discuss their condition with the parents but cannot do so themselves without permission from the competent child. The doctor could only legally inform the parents if it was found that the child was either not competent to consent to or refuse disclosure or that the refusal was not voluntary. The exception to this is when a young person (under 18) is refusing life-saving treatment. The doctor then has an overriding duty to inform those with parental responsibility who can then provide consent (see Chapter 4).

---

Box 8.5 **Confidentiality and contraception in children**

Prescribing the oral contraceptive pill to those under 16 is covered in Chapter 3. However, there are situations in which it is appropriate to breach the child's confidentiality:

- If the child is 12 or younger, anyone having sexual intercourse with her commits rape. Disclosure is at the clinical judgement of the healthcare professional but generally speaking, social services and possibly the police should be informed.

- Suspected emotional or sexual abuse should be reported to social services.

If neither of the situations applies, the child's confidentiality should be respected but the child should be encouraged to discuss the contraception with her parent(s).

---

The GMC also states that disclosure to an appropriate authority (social services or the police) should be undertaken (with or without the consent of the young person) if that young person is involved in behaviour such as joy-riding that might put the child or others at risk of serious harm.

If a parent is making decisions for a child who is not competent and disclosure is requested (for example, to allow clinical details to be used for research) then that parent's consent to the disclosure should be sought.

## Confidentiality and the deceased

There is no clear legal obligation of confidentiality to the deceased but the GMC and the Department of Health ethical guidelines state that the duty of confidentiality should continue to apply. However, information should be disclosed if requested by the coroner, for the death certificate, for National Confidential Enquiries and for public health surveillance. If information is disclosed for clinical audit or research, this information should be the minimum needed and anonymized where possible.

## The use of confidential records and X-rays in teaching, audit and research

### Audit and research

For the purposes of clinical audit, the team caring for the patient (but not other healthcare professionals) can look at the clinical records without express consent. However, if research other than audit is being undertaken, the specific consent of the patients to their notes being used for this purpose is required, irrespective of whether the researchers are part of the team looking after them or not. All healthcare professionals should only look at those parts of the record that are relevant to the research or audit and must anonymise the cases used. The records, whether electronic or paper, must be held securely.

If consent is not possible or has been withheld, but the research is thought to be in the public good then the research ethics committee should be consulted as normal. It will also be necessary to consult the PIAG with a view to using confidential records for the research under s251 of the NHS Act 2006 (see Box 8.1). The PIAG will assess whether the research merits a breach of confidentiality.

Case studies and photographs are invariably identifiable or potentially identifiable and the GMC advises that express consent to presentation or publication should be obtained. If the patient has died, the case should be anonymized as much as possible but can be presented or published, provided the deceased did not object and that publication would not cause distress to relatives.

## Teaching

Any patient-identifiable information (including pathology results, X-rays and other imaging) can only be used with the express consent of the patient. Otherwise teaching materials must be fully anonymized. Medical and other healthcare professional students are bound by a duty of confidentiality to the patients they encounter during their training.

## Access to confidential information by the police

The police have no general right of access to health records. However, under the Road Traffic Act 1988, the police have the power to require doctors to provide information that might identify a driver alleged to have committed a traffic offence. Where disclosure is required by a court or by statute, the minimum necessary should be disclosed. In reality, the patient often provides consent to disclosure, such as when a statement is required from the casualty doctor in cases of alleged assault. Requests for a blood sample from a patient are often made by the police. Box 8.6 summarizes the legal position.

---

**Box 8.6 Providing blood specimens for the police in an emergency**

Doctors may be asked by the police to take a blood sample for alcohol and drug testing in the Accident and Emergency Department from a patient who has been involved in a road traffic accident and who is unable to consent.

The Police Reform Act 2002 has clarified the doctor's duty in such a scenario. This gives a police officer the power to request that a blood sample be taken from a patient who is not competent to consent (usually because of impaired consciousness). This request may be made to a police surgeon or a medical practitioner who has no clinical responsibility for the care of the patient.

Complying with the request is not a legal requirement but it is lawful to do so. The doctor can refuse if it would be damaging to the clinical care of the patient to take the sample. It would not be lawful to take a blood sample from a patient who has capacity and has refused the blood sample. If a competent patient consents, the doctors can lawfully take the specimen if they feel it is clinically appropriate.

The sample will not be tested until the patient has regained capacity and gives consent. Again the relevant medical practitioner at the time will be notified of the intention to ask for consent and can object if this would adversely affect the care of the patient.

---

## Access to health records

### Handling confidential information

All healthcare information should be kept physically secure (Box 8.7). The Caldicott principles provide some guidance for handling such information:

1. Justify the purpose(s) of every disclosure
2. Do not use patient-identifiable information unless absolutely necessary
3. Use the minimum information necessary
4. Access to the information should be on a strict need-to-know basis
5. Everyone with access to such information should be aware of their responsibilities
6. Everyone with access to such information should understand and comply with the law.

---

**Box 8.7 Keeping information physically secure**

- Computers and patient notes should not be left in accessible areas (including an unattended car).
- Patient notes should not be taken home.
- Staff must always log out of a computer and never share logins or passwords (Figure 8.2).
- It is a criminal offence under the Computer Misuse Act 1980 for practitioners to access information on patients not under their care.

---

**Figure 8.2** Information must be secure. Never share logins or passwords.

- Patient information sent by e-mail should be anonymized or encrypted. It should not be sent via internet e-mails as these can be intercepted.
- Administration data should be kept and accessed separately from clinical data.

However, a doctor can show patients their healthcare records informally at any time. Patients (or their authorized representatives) also have a legal right to access their medical records under the Data Protection Act 1998. The request needs to be made to the data controller (in the medical records department) in writing and a fee may be charged. If information about medical issues is requested and the data controller is not a health professional then the information should not be provided unless a suitable health professional has been consulted. Under the Act, the patients also have the right to have any mistakes corrected on their health record. Children who are 12 or older and competent can access their medical records.

Under the Access to Medical Reports Act 1988, patients also have the right to see reports written about them for insurance or other purposes.

## Deceased patients

The Access to Health Records Act 1990 allows the deceased patient's personal representative and any person who may have a claim arising out of that patient's death to have access to the health records. The Act has otherwise been repealed since the enforcement of the Data Protection Act 1998.

**Case with key points: *X v Y* [1988] 2 All ER 648**

***Background***: A Health Authority employee gave the details of two GPs who had contracted human immunodeficiency virus (HIV) and who were still working to the press. The Health Authority sought to prevent the publication of the names of the doctors.

***Court Ruling***: The court ruled that although there is a public interest in the freedom of the press and some public interest in knowing the HIV status of the doctors, these are outweighed by the public interests in relation to loyalty and confidentiality in general and in relation to HIV patients in particular. The doctors' names should not be published.

***Key Points***: There is a balance that has to be ascertained in each case between the public interest in maintaining confidentiality and other public interests. In cases such as this, confidentiality is of paramount importance.

## Further reading

Children at risk of abuse: www.everychildmatters.gov.uk [2008]

Confidentiality: NHS Code of Practice 2003. www.dh.gov.uk/en/Publication sandstatistics/Publications/PublicationsPolicyAndGuidance/DH_4069253 [2008]

GMC: www.gmc-uk.org/guidance/current/library/confidentiality.asp [2008]

Medical conditions and driving: www.dvla.gov.uk/media/pdf/medical/aagv1.pdf [2008]

# CHAPTER 9

# Withholding and Withdrawing Life-Sustaining Treatment

*Lorraine Corfield*[1] *and Ingrid Granne*[2]

[1] Senior Vascular Fellow, Guy's and St Thomas' NHS Trust, London, UK
[2] Clinical Research Fellow and Specialist Registrar, Nuffield Department of Obstetrics and Gynaecology, University of Oxford, UK

> **OVERVIEW**
> - Competent adults (but not children) can refuse life-saving treatment.
> - Advance refusals can apply to life-saving treatment and must be respected if valid.
> - Euthanasia and assisted suicide are crimes.
> - A patient cannot demand futile treatment.

> Doctors have an ethical obligation to show respect for human life; protect the health of their patients; and to make their patients' best interests their first concern.
> – GMC: *Withholding and withdrawing life-prolonging treatments* (2002)

Healthcare professionals aim to improve the health and quality of life of their patients. This usually involves treating illness with a view to prolonging life. However, in some cases, active treatment may cause increased suffering or be more of a burden than a benefit. It will then be necessary to consider either not commencing life-saving treatment (withholding treatment) or stopping treatment that is already underway (withdrawing treatment).

The responsibility for such a decision lies with the senior clinician (Box 9.1). If this person is not available, the decision can be made by an experienced junior but must be discussed with the senior as soon as possible.

> Box 9.1 **When to seek advice**
>
> Healthcare professionals should consult a clinician or other relevant healthcare practitioners with the relevant experience if:
>
> - they have limited experience of the condition
> - they have doubts about the range of options
> - they are considering withdrawing artificial nutrition and hydration in a patient who is not imminently dying
> - there is a difference of opinion within the healthcare team that cannot be resolved by discussion (if this remains unsolved then legal advice should be sought).
>
> In general, consideration should always be given to obtaining a second opinion.

## Withholding and withdrawing treatment from competent adults

A competent adult can refuse any treatment, including life-saving treatment (see Chapter 4). In the case of *Re B* (Box 9.2) the court made it clear that a patient cannot be forced to try or continue with treatment even if healthcare professionals think it is in that patient's best interests to do so.

> Box 9.2 *Re B (adult: refusal of medical treatment)* (2002)
>
> A 44-year-old woman had suffered a cervical spinal cord haemorrhage. As a result she was tetraplegic and ventilator dependent. B requested that the ventilator be turned off. She rejected the options of a one-way weaning process (which had a probability of success of 1%) and rehabilitation on a spinal unit with a view to long-term ventilation. The court found that B was competent to make a decision to be removed from the ventilator. The fact that she had not experienced or tried rehabilitation did not affect her capacity to refuse this alternative. To continue to ventilate B against her competent wish was unlawful.

## Withholding and withdrawing treatment from incompetent adults

Life-prolonging treatment can be legally withheld or withdrawn from an incompetent patient if such treatment is not judged to be in their best interests and provided that the doctor complies with the terms of the Mental Capacity Act 2005 (see Chapter 2). Advance refusals (discussed in more detail in Chapter 4) do extend to life-sustaining treatment. In these cases, the advance refusal:

*ABC of Medical Law.* By Lorraine Corfield, Ingrid Granne and William Latimer-Sayer. Published 2009 by Blackwell Publishing, ISBN 978-1-4501-7628-6

- must be in writing
- must be signed and witnessed
- must clearly state that it applies if the person's life is at risk.

An advance refusal is valid unless overturned by the patient while still competent or unless the patient subsequently donates a lasting power of attorney (LPA) to another individual (who would then legally make the decision about withholding or withdrawing treatment). However, if the advance refusal was made *after* the donee of LPA was created then the advance refusal will stand. As with any advance refusal, the healthcare professional must assess whether the refusal is valid and applicable. Even if the refusal is not applicable, it should be considered by the treating healthcare team as part of their assessment of the best interests of the individual affected.

## Withholding and withdrawing treatment from children

In England, Wales and Northern Ireland, a person under the age of 18, whether competent or not, cannot refuse life-saving treatment. However, there may be situations in which providing or continuing such treatment will not be thought to be in the best interests of the child (such as where it is considered to be prolonging suffering with no prospect of improvement). This should be a decision made in conjunction with the child's parents. It is not surprising that there may be disagreement: this was highlighted in the well-publicized case of Charlotte Wyatt (*Wyatt v Portsmouth Hospitals NHS Trust* (2005)). Charlotte was born prematurely at 26 weeks and sustained severe brain, liver and kidney damage. The doctors in charge of her care felt that should she deteriorate further, artificial ventilation would not be in her best interests as she was blind, deaf and in constant pain. However, her parents disagreed: they felt that Charlotte had an appreciable quality of life and wanted her to be ventilated if necessary. The Court of Appeal ruled that although there is a strong presumption in favour of a course of action that will prolong life, that presumption is not absolute and the welfare of the child is paramount. The court conducted a balancing exercise in which all the relevant factors were weighed. On the facts of this particular case, the high court judge's decision that it would be lawful to withhold artificial ventilation was upheld by the Court of Appeal. If there is a non-resolved difference of opinion between parents and healthcare professionals, then legal advice must be sought.

## Withholding and withdrawing artificial nutrition and hydration

Artificial nutrition and hydration (ANH) is the provision of food or fluids by a route other than oral. It includes nasogastric or nasojejunal feeding, feeding by a percutaneous endoscopic gastrostomy or feeding jejunostomy, peripheral or central parenteral nutrition and subcutaneous or intravenous fluids. It is a controversial area as all of these methods are invasive and carry varying degrees of risk that may outweigh any potential benefit.

Advance refusals do extend to the withdrawal or withholding of ANH, provided the criteria given here for advance refusals of life-sustaining treatment are fulfilled. However, they do not extend to the offer of oral fluids and food as this is seen legally as part of basic care.

The judgment in *Burke* (see case with key points) gave further legal guidance on the provision of ANH:

- withdrawing ANH from a patient who requires it to live against the express wishes of that patient is an infringement of Article 2 (the right to life) of the Human Rights Act 1998 and leaves the doctor open to a charge of murder
- where ANH is needed to keep a patient alive, the doctor will normally be under a duty of care to provide it (but the doctor is not obliged to do so if providing ANH is clinically futile or not in best interests of the incompetent patient)
- a healthcare professional cannot withdraw ANH from a patient who expresses the wish to remain alive.

It is not necessary to obtain a court ruling for the withdrawing or withholding of ANH unless the patient is in a permanent vegetative state. The Mental Capacity Act 2005 in England, Wales and Northern Ireland does not change the common law position following the case of *Airedale NHS Trust v Bland* (1993). This requires that an application be made to court to determine what should be done. In Scotland, however, there is no requirement to go to court even in cases of permanent vegetative state but nonetheless, legal advice should be sought.

## Do not resuscitate orders

As with withholding other life-saving treatments, a competent patient's refusal to accept cardiopulmonary resuscitation (CPR) must legally be respected. The same is true of a patient lacking capacity with a valid, written, signed, witnessed and applicable advance refusal for CPR. Healthcare providers should usually comply with a competent patient's request for CPR to be undertaken but, as with all treatment, there is no obligation to provide treatment that is clinically futile. If the patient is not competent and there is no advance refusal, then the decision over resuscitation must be based on an assessment of best interests (as governed by the Mental Capacity Act 2005; see Chapter 2) (Figure 9.1).

The decision should be made in advance where possible and it should be clear to patients, relatives and the healthcare team that it applies to CPR and not active treatment in general unless otherwise specified. Any 'do not resuscitate' (DNR) order should be reviewed regularly and the decision made should comply with the relevant hospital protocols. The resuscitation council has provided guidance if no clear plan is in place and an arrest occurs (Box 9.3).

> **Box 9.3 Resuscitation council guidelines**
>
> The Resuscitation Council states that if there is no resuscitation plan and the wishes of the patient are unknown, resuscitation should generally be initiated. However, there may be situations where resuscitation may be inappropriate:
>
> - CPR is unlikely to be successful.
> - Cardiopulmonary arrest is an anticipated terminal event.

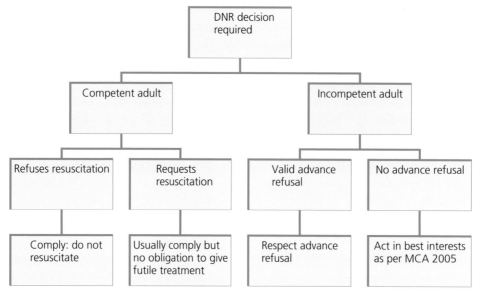

**Figure 9.1** Flow chart guiding 'do not resuscitate' (DNR) decisions in adults.

- Successful CPR is likely to be followed by a quality of life that is not in the best interests of the patient.
- There is a valid advance refusal of CPR (CPR must not be undertaken in this situation).

The responsibility for a DNR decision rests with the senior clinician (or occasionally a nurse specialist or nurse consultant in palliative care, for example). It is not necessary to initiate a discussion about CPR if there is reason to believe that it is unlikely that the patient will suffer a cardiac arrest. If the patient does not wish to discuss the issue, this should not be forced on them.

A DNR decision does not override clinical judgement in an unexpected arrest with a reversible cause (such as choking, blocked tracheostomy or arrest on induction of anaesthesia). The order can be temporarily suspended and the decision to resuscitate made at the time of any arrest. For example, an elderly patient with metastatic caecal cancer is undergoing a bowel resection to prevent obstruction. There is a DNR order in place but she has a sudden episode of ventricular fibrillation during anaesthesia. If the medical team think that this is likely to be reversible and that treating the arrhythmia is in her best interests, it would be lawful to defibrillate the patient (unless she has specifically refused resuscitation in this circumstance).

### DNR decisions and incompetent adults

The Mental Capacity Act 2005 should be applied here as for any clinical decision (see Chapter 2). If a patient lacks the capacity to

decide about CPR and there is nobody appropriate to consult, it may be necessary to consider instructing an independent mental capacity advocate (IMCA) (see Chapter 2 for further details about the IMCA service). An IMCA will not be needed if there is a clear clinical decision that resuscitation is futile. However, IMCAs should generally be instructed for serious medical decisions or decisions with serious consequences for the patient (unless the decision is clinically urgent). The law is not clear as to whether CPR is one such decision but there are obviously serious consequences to a DNR order (or to undertaking CPR). Seeking legal advice as to the need to instruct an IMCA is advised should this situation arise.

Asking the parents of a sick child to sign a DNR form may well increase distress and is not legally necessary.

## Conscientious objection

If a healthcare practitioner has a conscientious objection to withholding or withdrawing treatment (once this decision has been made by a competent adult or senior clinician), that practitioner can withdraw from the care of the patient but must ensure that another colleague takes over without delay. Junior members of the team must inform their senior as soon as possible of their objection.

## The doctor and euthanasia

The law is clear that where a healthcare professional's *primary* intention is to bring about death, whatever the motivation, to do so would amount to the criminal charge of murder.

|  | Euthanasia | Assisted suicide |
|---|---|---|
| Definition | The deliberate act of ending a patient's life *Voluntary euthanasia* is undertaken at the request of the competent patient *Non-voluntary euthanasia* is the 'mercy-killing' of incompetent patients when this is thought to be in their best interests | In assisted suicide, a competent person makes the decision that they wish to commit suicide but cannot do so unaided. The patient performs the final fatal act but the healthcare professional provides the means by which to commit suicide |
| Example | Injecting suffering patients with potassium chloride with the intention of killing them | Providing a massive dose of barbiturates to a patient in the knowledge that they intend to overdose |
| Legal position | All forms of euthanasia are legally murder | Aiding and abetting suicide is a crime under the Suicide Act 1961 |

## Can a patient demand life-sustaining treatment?

Although doctors have a duty to discuss possible treatment options with a competent patient and respect that patient's autonomous decision, a patient cannot demand a treatment that is clinically futile or adverse to his clinical needs. This was clarified recently by the Court of Appeal in the case of Leslie Burke (see case with key points).

### Case with key points: *Burke v GMC* [2005] EWCA Civ 1003

*Background*: Leslie Burke was a 45-year-old man suffering from the physically degenerative condition spinocerebellar ataxia. He had retained his mental capacity and was likely to do so throughout his illness. Mr Burke was concerned that when he became unable to swallow doctors may feel that artificial nutrition and hydration would not be in his interests and it would be withheld, thus inflicting discomfort from starvation.

*Court ruling*: A patient cannot demand specific medical treatment at any time, including by advance directive.

*Key points*: A doctor who deliberately stops life-sustaining treatment against the express wishes of a competent patient would have to answer to a charge of murder. This ruling does not change the doctor's duty to discuss reasonable treatment options with his patient. There is no legal duty for a doctor to offer or provide futile treatment. A person can state his wishes in advance: healthcare professionals will be bound to consider these if at some point in the future it becomes necessary to assess best interests.

## Further reading

BMA. *Decisions Relating to Cardiopulmonary Resuscitation.* www.bma.org.uk/ health_promotion_ethics/cardiopulmonary_resuscitation/ CPRDecisions07.jsp [2009]

British Medical Association, Resuscitation Council (UK), Royal College of Nursing. *Decisions Relating to Cardiopulmonary Resuscitation.* Joint statement from the British Medical Association, the Resuscitation Council (UK) and the Royal College of Nursing, October 2007. www.resus.org.uk/ pages/dnar.pdf [2008]

GMC. *Withholding and Withdrawing Life-Prolonging Treatments: Good Practice in Decision-Making.* (2002) www.gmc-uk.org/guidance/current/ library/witholding_lifeprolonging_guidance.asp [2008]

Resuscitation Council Guidelines. www.resus.org.uk/pages/standard.pdf [2008]

# CHAPTER 10

# Research

*Lorraine Corfield[1], Ruth Wilkinson[2] and Ingrid Granne[3]*

[1] Senior Vascular Fellow, Guy's and St Thomas' NHS Trust, London, UK
[2] Centre for Social Ethics and Policy, Institute for Science, Ethics and Innovation, School of Law, University of Manchester, UK
[3] Clinical Research Fellow and Specialist Registrar, Nuffield Department of Obstetrics and Gynaecology, University of Oxford, UK

---

### OVERVIEW

- Consent to participating in research must be competent, voluntary and informed.

- Competent adults can consent to any reasonable research: special arrangements are necessary for children and incompetent adults.

- Written information should be provided to all research participants.

- Healthcare professionals should not commence research without the approval of a research ethics committee.

---

Research involving people directly or indirectly is vital in improving care and reducing uncertainty for patients now and in the future, and improving the health of the population as a whole.
    – GMC: *Good Medical Practice* (2006)

Many healthcare professionals undertake research in one form or another. This may be via a formal research degree, a project as part of a degree, research during clinical posts or recruiting patients for trials. This chapter will give an overview of the law in this area but refers to research on human subjects only. Any professional wishing to set up a major trial, research involving animals, human embryos, gene therapy or xenotransplantation will need to seek further advice.

The law, particularly case law, on research is less prolific than in many other areas and thus much is extrapolated from the law regarding medical treatment in general. There are three main legal considerations in medical research: consent, duty of care to the patient and confidentiality. Confidentiality in research is covered in Chapter 8.

## Consent

As with consent to any medical treatment, for consent to participation in research to be valid, the individual giving consent must

be competent (have the capacity to consent) and the consent must be both voluntary and informed. For research, the consent should always be written. If that is not possible, an oral witnessed consent should be obtained.

## Therapeutic and non-therapeutic research

Research is considered to be *therapeutic* if the participants are patients receiving some form of treatment, albeit experimental (such as a cancer patient in a trial of a novel chemotherapy treatment), in which the foreseeable risks do not outweigh the potential benefits. Research is *non-therapeutic* if the participants are patients or healthy volunteers who have no prospect of a direct health benefit from the research. The risks in non-therapeutic research must be kept to the absolute minimum possible. Most healthcare professionals engaged in non-therapeutic research will be undertaking retrospective reviews or non-medicinal research (such as the effect of exercise on cardiovascular parameters). However, such research also includes phase 1 clinical trials (such as that of the monoclonal antibody drug TGN 1412 on six healthy men in 2006, which resulted in unexpected and serious immunocompromise in the six volunteers).

## Clinical trials involving medicinal products

The Medicines for Human Use (Clinical Trials) Regulations 2004 govern how research undertaken to assess the efficacy or safety of a medicinal product should be conducted (Box 10.1). To be lawful, such clinical trials (clinical trials of investigational medicinal products (CTIMPs) must comply with these regulations and must be approved by the Medicines and Healthcare Products Regulatory Agency (MHRA). In addition, the proposed trial must receive ethical approval from a recognized research ethics committee. Researchers can apply to recognized committees through the usual ethics committee application process.

---

Box 10.1 **What is a medicinal product for the purposes of a CTIMP?**

- Any substance administered for the treatment or investigation of a medical disorder or for medical purposes
- Does not include human whole blood, blood cells or plasma

---

*ABC of Medical Law.* By Lorraine Corfield, Ingrid Granne
and William Latimer-Sayer. Published 2009 by Blackwell Publishing,
ISBN 978-1-4501-7628-6

- Does not include tissues, unless they are a somatic cell therapy
- Does not include cosmetic products or food (such as dietary supplements) that are not presented as medicines
- Does not include medical devices.

If any doubt exists as to whether the trial involves a medicinal product, the MHRA should be contacted.

## Consent in research: capacity
### Clinical trials involving medicinal products

The basic legal position on consent in CTIMPs is summarized in Figure 10.1.

- Competent adults and 16 and 17 year olds can be enrolled in a CTIMP with their valid consent.
- Incompetent adults can participate with some safeguards: the consent of a legal representative not connected with the research project is required. The clinical trials regulations state that for incompetent adults to take part in therapeutic medicinal research there must be a direct relationship between the research and the life-threatening or debilitating clinical condition from which they suffer (for example, the area of research should be Alzheimer's disease rather than a co-existent condition such as diabetes or heart failure).
- Children (under 16) can only be involved in therapeutic medicinal research with parental consent, irrespective of the child's capacity and understanding (although it is possible that a competent child may be able to consent: if the situation arises where consent of the child without parental consent is thought to be appropriate then legal advice should be sought). Medicinal research can be carried out on a minor only if it is in direct relation to a condition from which the minor suffers.

### Non-medicinal therapeutic research

This includes some randomized and prospective studies. An example would be a randomized study comparing open and laparoscopic surgery. The basic legal position on consent for such studies is summarized in Figure 10.2.

- Competent adults (18 and over) can be enrolled with their valid consent.
- The capacity of possibly incompetent adults should be assessed as per the Mental Capacity Act 2005 (MCA; see Chapter 2). If a non-medicinal therapeutic research study requires the involvement of incompetent adults, the MCA imposes several legal requirements (Box 10.2).
- Parental consent is needed on behalf of all children in relation to proposed therapeutic research (including 16 and 17 year olds: if consent from the minor alone is thought to be appropriate legal advice is recommended). However, the child's wishes should always be taken into account and it would be unusual to proceed without the agreement of a child (if the child is old enough to understand what is taking place).

Box 10.2 **Legal requirements when involving incompetent adults in non-medicinal therapeutic research**

- A research ethics committee must be consulted.
- The research must have a potential benefit to the patient without imposing a burden to them that is disproportionate to the benefit.
- The research must be related to the impairment of the mind or brain that underlies their inability to consent.
- Another person must be consulted (an unpaid carer or someone interested in the incompetent adult's welfare) and the views of other relevant individuals must be taken into account. If an appropriate consultee cannot be found, the researchers must identify someone unconnected with the research to act on behalf of the incompetent adult.
- The objections of the person lacking capacity must be respected: the research cannot be undertaken or, if in progress, must cease if the incompetent person becomes distressed or objects.
- Advance refusals must be respected.

### Non-therapeutic research

This includes retrospective studies, such as reviewing the complications of a certain treatment. As mentioned earlier, it also

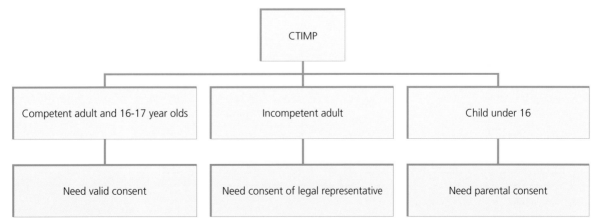

**Figure 10.1** Consent in CTIMPS: how to proceed.

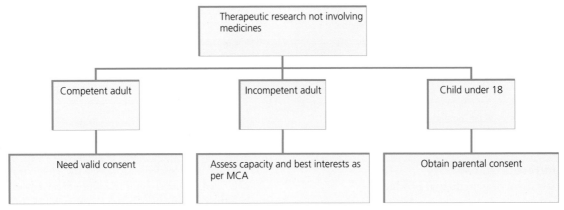

**Figure 10.2** Consent in therapeutic research not involving medicines: how to proceed (MCA: Mental Capacity Act 2005).

includes phase one trials of new medicinal products. The basic legal position on consent for non-therapeutic research is summarized in Figure 10.3.

- Competent adults can participate in non-therapeutic research if they provide valid consent. If medicinal products are involved, then 16- and 17-year-olds can consent for themselves. For all other non-therapeutic research, parental consent is required until the child reaches 18.
- Incompetent adults pose many problems in non-therapeutic research. There are no clear differences in the law between medicinal and non-medicinal non-therapeutic research. It is difficult to justify non-therapeutic research involving incompetent adults, and any researchers considering embarking on this type of study should seek legal advice.
- The Clinical Trials Regulations make it very difficult to enrol children (under 16) in non-therapeutic medicinal research, although the possibility is provided for in very narrow circumstances. If such research projects are felt to be necessary then legal advice is essential. For non-therapeutic non-medicinal research parents can consent but it would be sensible to seek legal advice for this type of trial.

## Consent in research: voluntariness

Healthcare professionals must be aware that when asking a patient for consent to participate in research, the patient may feel (consciously or subconsciously) that they owe it to the healthcare professional to participate. This may be due to the clinical relationship or because the patient fears that their future treatment may suffer. Every effort should be made to reassure the patient that the latter is not the case and that there is no onus on them to consent: the relationship between healthcare professional and patient will not be affected. If there is a real suspicion that consent may not be voluntary then the patient should not be included in the study. In any event, it may be more appropriate for the initial approach to be made by a person not involved in the clinical care of the patient.

Many patients, particularly those with chronic or fatal illness, will be desperate and will consent to any treatment offered, whether it is part of a research study or not. Those recruiting should ensure as much as possible that this does not affect the validity of the consent and that such patients are realistic about any prospect of improvement in their condition. As with consent for any medical procedure, relatives may, intentionally or otherwise, be coercive,

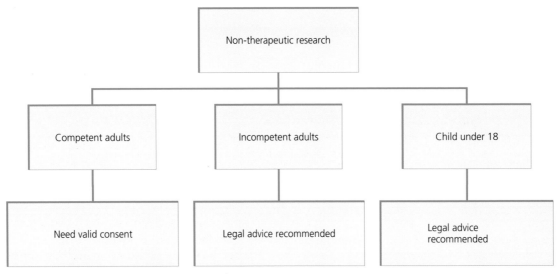

**Figure 10.3** Consent in non-therapeutic research: how to proceed.

particularly for a dying relative to agree to participate in research in the hope of a cure (Box 10.3).

---

Box 10.3 **Individuals who may be particularly vulnerable to implicit coercion**

- Students of the professional or department conducting the research
- Junior colleagues
- Long-standing loyal patients
- Terminally ill patients
- Prisoners (in the hope of earlier release).

---

Offering financial rewards for participating in research has a major effect on voluntariness and is unacceptable. Volunteers and patients (including children or their parents and carers of incompetent adults) can be reimbursed for their time and travel but no inducement above this should be offered. Reimbursement should not be related to the degree of any risk involved.

## Consent in research: information

For consent to be legally valid, as for any procedure or treatment, the individual must be informed about what is intended and why (Box 10.4). The research purpose must be made very clear even where there is also an intention to treat (therapeutic research). The potential benefits and risks must also be explained. Subjects not informed of foreseeable risks may be able to claim in negligence if such a risk should eventuate. The legal standard for risk disclosure in non-therapeutic research (where the subject has no chance of a medical benefit) is likely to be very high. Providing written information for all research is good practice to ensure that the appropriate information is disclosed. In any event, a research ethics committee will require a written information sheet before approving a research proposal involving human participants (Box 10.5).

---

Box 10.4 *Halushska v University of Saskatchewan* **(1965) 52 WWR 608**

A student seeking employment was asked to participate in research at his own university for $50. He was told by the doctors involved that it was a safe test during which a catheter would be inserted into a vein of his left arm. The student signed a consent form absolving the doctors of any responsibility in the event of an adverse event. The research actually involved passing the catheter through the heart into the pulmonary artery. This had not been disclosed to the student. During the test the student suffered a cardiac arrest and required open heart massage via a thoracotomy.

The Canadian court found that for the purposes of research a full and frank disclosure of the entire procedure and possible risks is essential. There is no role for therapeutic privilege or withholding details of the procedure. Signing a consent form absolving the researchers of responsibility was of no relevance if, as here, there was a negligent failure to provide information.

(The relevance of Canadian cases to English law is discussed in Chapter 1).

---

Box 10.5 **Additional information required in consent for research**

- Sources of funding
- Trial procedures, including a clear description of what this means for the individual participant
- Method of any randomization and explanation of the notion of randomization
- The use of any placebo or control group, explaining that the participant may be placed in such a group
- The ability of the participant to withdraw at any time without prejudicing their ongoing care
- The responsibilities of the participant
- Any available treatment alternatives outside the trial
- The anticipated length of the trial
- The number of subjects
- Whether the results may be published
- Confidentiality arrangements
- The institutional affiliations of the researchers
- Indemnity and insurance provisions
- Any provision for aftercare.

---

## The duty of care in research and best interests

As discussed in relation to medical treatment, healthcare professionals have a duty of care to their patients. The duty of care in relation to research requires professionals to be sure that the participants understand the details of the consent, and that the consent given is valid. If a patient does not understand, or cannot accept, randomization and the possibility of receiving a placebo, then the professional should not enrol the patient in the proposed research. To try to protect the best interests of the patient when involved in research the healthcare professional must:

- ensure that medical care is not compromised should the patient withdraw from the research and that the patient is aware of this
- answer any questions the participant has truthfully and openly
- be aware that some adults, even if competent, can still be vulnerable (including the elderly or very unwell). These people may need the support of a relative, for example, if involved in research
- report any concern that a person is being put at risk by the research.

Further good practice points are given in Box 10.6

---

Box 10.6 **Further good practice points**

- Research projects should be completed by the original researchers, or they should do their best to ensure that the projects are completed by others.
- Results should be published whenever possible, preferably in a peer-reviewed journal.

- The participants and the research ethics committee (REC) may be interested in the research findings; consider sending a brief statement of the findings after the research is complete.
- All authors must have contributed to the article or the research.
- Fraud must be reported.
- Any funding or conflict of interest should be declared to all involved, including participants.

## Research ethics committees

In addition to the legal requirements, research is regulated by, and approval must be sought from, the relevant research ethics committee (REC) (Box 10.7) before commencing the study (Figure 10.4). If such approval is not sought, it will not be possible to publish the findings in a reputable peer-reviewed journal and there may be repercussions from the General Medical Council or relevant professional regulatory body. For research involving human tissue,

incompetent adults or medicines, there may be legal ramifications if prior approval is not sought from the REC.

Box 10.7 **The role of research ethics committees**

The National Research Ethics Service (NRES) plays a crucial dual role in the governance of research within the NHS. It is the duty of the NRES to protect the 'safety, dignity and well-being of research participants, whilst facilitating and promoting ethical research within the NHS'. Committees are made up of both lay people and medical professionals. Researchers must complete an integrated research application system (IRAS) form describing their proposed research, which an ethics committee will scrutinize before approving or rejecting the study (Figure 10.5).

Standard practice is for researchers to send a description of their proposed research to their closest REC. However, if another REC has more appropriate expertise, or meets sooner, for example, researchers may apply to a different REC.

RECs only review the ethical aspects and implications of proposed research projects. The science should be reviewed separately and this

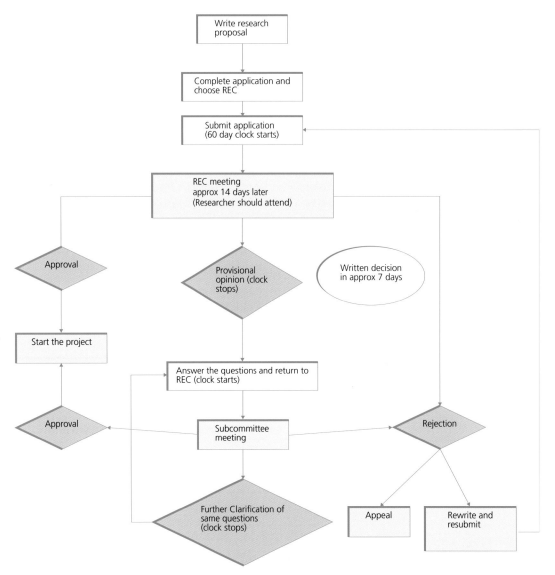

**Figure 10.4** The REC process.

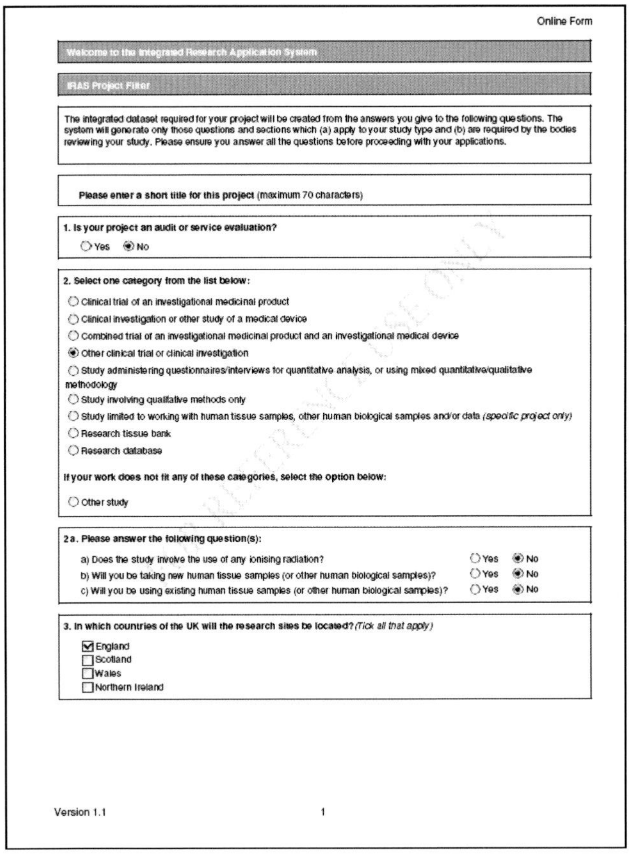
Online Form

Welcome to the Integrated Research Application System

IRAS Project Filter

The integrated dataset required for your project will be created from the answers you give to the following questions. The system will generate only those questions and sections which (a) apply to your study type and (b) are required by the bodies reviewing your study. Please ensure you answer all the questions before proceeding with your applications.

**Please enter a short title for this project** (maximum 70 characters)

**1. Is your project an audit or service evaluation?**

Yes / No

**2. Select one category from the list below:**

Clinical trial of an investigational medicinal product
Clinical investigation or other study of a medical device
Combined trial of an investigational medicinal product and an investigational medical device
Other clinical trial or clinical investigation
Study administering questionnaires/interviews for quantitative analysis, or using mixed quantitative/qualitative methodology
Study involving qualitative methods only
Study limited to working with human tissue samples, other human biological samples and/or data *(specific project only)*
Research tissue bank
Research database

**If your work does not fit any of these categories, select the option below:**

Other study

**2a. Please answer the following question(s):**

a) Does the study involve the use of any ionising radiation? Yes No
b) Will you be taking new human tissue samples (or other human biological samples)? Yes No
c) Will you be using existing human tissue samples (or other human biological samples)? Yes No

**3. In which countries of the UK will the research sites be located?** *(Tick all that apply)*

England
Scotland
Wales
Northern Ireland

Version 1.1 1

**Figure 10.5** The integrated research application system online form.

is likely to be required as part of the application process. There may be legally qualified people on an REC but this is not a requirement. The REC does not address the legality of the research: this is the responsibility of the researcher (who should seek legal advice as appropriate).

## Research in emergency situations

Research projects may involve emergency treatment (such as the use of a drug in a trial setting in head injury patients). As a result of the nature of the emergency (such as a reduced Glasgow Coma Score), the individual may not be able to provide consent to participate in the trial. There may not be time to adhere to the usual channels for involving incompetent individuals in research. It may be possible to go ahead if the research is *therapeutic* provided that:

- any advance refusal is respected
- the treatment is given only if immediately necessary
- the treatment is discussed with the next of kin wherever possible
- consent is obtained as soon as possible.

Ethics committee approval must also have been obtained in advance and these issues clarified before the research commencing. The REC will usually require a specific procedure for obtaining consent after the emergency has passed and a commitment that all data provided by a participant will be destroyed if that participant later refuses to be involved in the study.

## Audit

It is good practice for all healthcare professionals to participate in clinical audit. This involves undertaking local audit projects as well as complying with ongoing local and national audit projects. All audit projects should be registered with the relevant audit department and results should be made available to the same department. Ethics committees cannot consider audit projects. Confidentiality issues in audit are discussed in Chapter 8.

**Case with key points: *Simms v Simms* [2002] EWHC 2734 (Fam)**

***Background***: Two teenagers (aged 16 and 18) were dying from variant Creutzfeldt–Jakob disease. Neither patient had capacity to decide about a proposed experimental treatment which had never been tested in humans. Their parents sought a court declaration that an intracerebral infusion treatment from Japan, which inhibited prion formation in mice, could lawfully be made available to their children.

***Court decision***: The court held that this was innovative treatment, not research, and that it could be lawfully administered. Although the Bolam test could not be fulfilled to its fullest extent as the treatment was innovative, a small group of specialists satisfied the judge that there was a relevant body of medical opinion supporting the use of the treatment. The court also found that the patients' Article 2 and 8 rights (the right to life and the right to respect for family life: see Chapter 12) weighed in favour of treatment.

***Key Points***: Innovative treatment differs from research in that the aim is purely therapeutic, despite its novelty. If there is no realistic treatment alternative for a fatal illness, there is no significant risk of increasing suffering and there is some chance of benefit, then giving the innovative treatment can be lawful. Obviously, this should be undertaken with consent or by adhering to the law on consent if the patient is a child or incompetent adult. The procedure or drug should have been tested as much as possible up to the point of being administered to a patient, and there must be careful monitoring for harm.

## Further reading


General Medical Council. *Research: The Role and Responsibilities of Doctors*, 2002 at www.gmc-uk.org/guidance/current/library/research.asp [2008]

International Conference on Harmonisation. *Guideline for Good Clinical Practice*, 1996 at www.ich.org/cache/compo/475-272-1.html#E6 [2008]

Medicines and Healthcare Products Regulatory Agency at www.mhra.gov.uk [2008]

Medicines for Human Use Regulations 2004, http://www.opsi.gov.uk/si/si2004/20041031.htm [2008]

Mental Capacity Act Code of Practice at www.dca.gov.uk/menincap/legis.htm [2008]

National Research Ethics Service at www.nres.npsa.nhs.uk [2008]

# CHAPTER 11

# Organ Transplantation, Organ Retention and Post-Mortem Examinations

*Ruth Wilkinson[1], Lorraine Corfield[2] and Ingrid Granne[3]*

[1]Centre for Social Ethics and Policy, Institute for Science, Ethics and Innovation, School of Law, University of Manchester, UK
[2]Senior Vascular Fellow, Guy's and St Thomas' NHS Trust, London, UK
[3]Clinical Research Fellow and Specialist Registrar, Nuffield Department of Obstetrics and Gynaecology, University of Oxford, UK

---

## OVERVIEW

- Both cadaveric and live organ donation for transplantation are lawful in the United Kingdom.

- Tissues and organs can only be retained (for any reason) with appropriate consent.

- Deaths in many circumstances (including where the cause of death is unknown) must be reported to the coroner who has the power to order a post-mortem.

- Non-coroner (hospital) post-mortems can only be undertaken with consent (usually from the next of kin).

---

Organ transplantation is an accepted and integral therapy for organ failure. Organ transplantation improves life expectancy and quality of life of the individual and their family.

– British Transplantation Society: *Standards for Solid Organ Transplantation in the United Kingdom*

The organ retention scandals at Bristol and Liverpool in the early 1990s resulted in increased controversy over the use and retention of human tissue and organs. Organ transplantation raises further debate. While there is a great deal of support for organ donation programs across the United Kingdom, when it comes to the crunch many people are either not asked or are reluctant to agree to donation. This is a very difficult situation: considerable numbers of patients will die without a transplant but the organs of suitable donors fail to be transplanted. The reasons for refusal range from the spiritual or religious to the pragmatic: relatives may be asked at an inappropriate time, or in an inappropriate manner. This is an extremely sensitive area for healthcare professionals: there is a fairly small window of opportunity to ask for an organ to be donated, which must be used without appearing callous and unsympathetic. Knowing what the law allows and requires should make this difficult process easier for all involved.

*ABC of Medical Law*. By Lorraine Corfield, Ingrid Granne
and William Latimer-Sayer. Published 2009 by Blackwell Publishing,
ISBN 978-1-4501-7628-6

## Organ donation and transplantation

### Cadaveric donors

To be a suitable organ donor, a number of criteria must be met. The first and most obvious is that the organs must be healthy, which rules out many who have died from, or with, conditions such as disseminated malignancy. An ideal candidate is someone who has suffered fatal head injuries but with no harm to the rest of their organs. The donor should also be free of any infectious disease that may injure the health of the recipient. For example, a human immunodeficiency virus (HIV) test on the donor must be negative, although this should be supported by inquiries into whether the donor had undertaken any high-risk sexual activity or ever injected drugs.

Secondly, the donor must be dead. This is not as simple as it sounds. In the United Kingdom, there is no legal definition of death. The development of artificial ventilators has made it very difficult to ascertain when someone has actually died, since the cessation of heart and lung function is no longer sufficient. The Department of Health recommends brain stem death (the irreversible cessation of brain stem function) to be the appropriate measure and this has been accepted as a valid diagnosis of death by British courts. The diagnosis of brain stem death must be made by two medical practitioners who have been qualified for 5 or more years. At least one must be a consultant and both must be competent in this area but neither should be a member of the transplant team: The practice of ventilating a patient purely to allow donation is discussed in Box 11.1.

---

### Box 11.1 **Elective ventilation**

This is the practice of artificially ventilating a patient before death (such as from unsurvivable head trauma) for no purpose other than to obtain organs for transplantation. It is not clear whether elective ventilation is lawful in the United Kingdom. It would seem that since the ventilation is not being carried out for the benefit of the patient it would violate the doctor's duty to act in the patient's best interests. However, it has been argued that elective ventilation is *not against* the interests of the patient and therefore it is not unlawful. Indeed, doctors from one English NHS Trust have published data from their experience of elective ventilation over several years.

---

Thirdly, there must be appropriate consent for the removal of the organs. Since September 2006, this has been governed by the

Human Tissue Act 2004 (HTA). Appropriate consent means the consent of:

(1) the donor themselves before death or
(2) a donee of the donor's lasting power of attorney (see Chapter 2), if one has been appointed or
(3) someone in a qualifying relationship to the donor:
  - spouse or partner
  - parent or child
  - brother or sister
  - grandparent or grandchild
  - child of a brother or sister
  - stepfather or stepmother
  - half-brother or half-sister
  - friend of long standing.

This list is strictly hierarchical. Consent must be sought from the person in the highest possible position (Figure 11.1). If a potential donor has made it clear before death that they wish to be donors then it is lawful to retrieve their organs. This means that if the deceased carried a donor card, or is on the organ donor register then they have consented to donate their organs. It is then not legally necessary to obtain the consent of relatives although a discussion with the next of kin if available would generally be appropriate. If the deceased has made it clear that they do not want to donate their organs then this also stands. The system for consenting to donation varies between countries (Box 11.2). Where children are the potential donors the consent requirements are very similar. Appropriate consent is rarely given in advance by the children themselves so someone with parental responsibility or someone in a qualifying relationship to the children must be consulted.

---

Box 11.2 **How could the supply of organs be increased? Opt-in and opt-out systems**

In the United Kingdom, there are enough potential organ donors to meet the demand for organs. The shortage in organs arises because only half of these potential donors become actual donors. 'Opt-in' systems, such as that which operates in the United Kingdom at the moment (Figure 11.2), require people to specifically choose to become an organ donor.

Opt-out systems are common in Europe. The system works on the principle that consent is given to donate, unless it is specifically withdrawn. These systems may include a right for the relatives to veto the donation, but the strict rule is that unless individuals have specifically refused in advance, they are willing to donate their organs after their death.

---

## Live organ donation

The legal rules covering the donation of organs from living persons are found in common law and in statute law (the Human Tissue Act 2004).

In the United Kingdom, organs can lawfully be donated between genetic relatives, emotional relatives (such as a spouse or step-parent) and complete strangers. Genetic and emotional relatives make directed donations, meaning that the organs are to go to a specific recipient. Where the donor is not suitable to donate to the specified recipient the couple can be matched to another donor and recipient so that both recipients can receive suitable organs. Donations by complete strangers are non-directed and can be domino donations or entirely altruistic donations. Domino donations occur when the donation is being carried out for the medical benefit of the donor. It is sometimes easier to transplant heart and lungs rather than lungs alone. When a patient needs a lung transplant, they may receive heart and lungs from a cadaveric donor and their heart may then be donated to another recipient. The Human Tissue Act 2004 also allows purely altruistic donation between complete strangers. This is non-directed donation, and all potential donors must be interviewed by an independent psychiatrist. All proposed living donor transplants must be approved by independent assessors accredited by the Human Tissue Authority.

## Requirements for consent in live organ donation

Organ donation is made possible by the principle that all adults are considered to be autonomous. The general rule is that an adult is

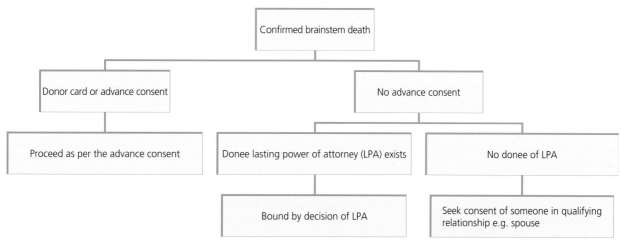

**Figure 11.1** Consent hierarchy for organ donation.

**We've signed up. Have you?**

Join the NHS Organ Donor Register

**Figure 11.2** The United Kingdom has an 'opt-in' system for donated organs.

presumed competent to consent to an organ being removed for the purposes of transplantation.

### Valid consent for donation

As discussed in Chapter 2, the basis for a valid consent is that it is voluntary, informed and given by a competent person. The main concern in this situation is voluntariness. When donations are made between family members, which will often be the case, it can be difficult to be sure that the decision to donate has been made without coercion or undue influence. This can be overt but may also be more subtle: the potential donor may feel a sense of duty, particularly if they are the only family member who is a match. They may also fear for their future family relationships should they not donate.

### What can an adult choose to donate?

The legal principle that a person cannot consent to an act that amounts to actual bodily harm applies in relation to organ donation. So, living donors cannot donate their heart, whole lungs or both their kidneys. Currently, the law allows living donors to donate regenerative tissue, and any non-regenerative tissue that is not essential to life. This means one kidney, a lobe of lung or a section of liver.

### The Human Tissue Act 2004

The Human Tissue Act 2004 (HTA) created the criminal offence of using an organ for transplantation without the appropriate

consent of the donor. The Human Tissue Authority's Code of Practice on Donation of Organs states that written rather than verbal consent should be sought and that the consent process should be part of an ongoing dialogue that starts well in advance of the intended procedure. Surgeons should continue to ensure that the donor still consents right up until the surgery takes place. The HTA continues the ban on the sale of organs (Box 11.3).

---

**Box 11.3 Payment for organs**

It is an offence to buy, sell, offer to buy or sell or to arrange the sale of an organ for transplantation. The offence is committed by both the buyer and the seller, and anyone who arranges an organ sale. The maximum sentence for this offence is 3 years in prison. This provision does not prevent the payment of expenses (travel and loss of earnings) to living donors but payments cannot be related to the loss of the organ.

**Could there be a commercial market in organs?**

Many reasons are cited for the ban on commercial sale of organs in the United Kingdom. The most important are as follows:

- There is something intrinsically wrong with the commodification of the human body.
- Organ donation should be altruistic and selling organs undermines this principle.
- Money can be coercive and may invalidate a person's consent.
- In a free market, an organ would be sold to the highest bidder: this undermines equality in healthcare by limiting the poor's access to organs.

---

### Incompetent adults and children

The law here is essentially the same as that regarding treating minors and incompetent adults. The HTA does allow both incompetent adults and children to be organ donors if it is in their own best interests.

In the case of children, consent is needed from someone with parental responsibility, and doctors would be advised to get consent from both parents. The *Gillick* rules have not been extended to organ transplantation, but the HTA does not rule out organ donation from a competent child. Where a child appears competent to consent to organ donation, it would be good practice to get parental consent as well. Once consent has been given the case must be referred to the Human Tissue Authority for approval.

For incompetent adults, the Mental Capacity Act 2005 requires that once an adult has been found to be incompetent, any treatment given must be in their best interests. Any proposed donation must be scrutinized and approved by the Human Tissue Authority, which has indicated in its Code of Practice that it will only consider these cases if a court has already approved them. Cases involving potential donation from incompetent adults must therefore be brought before the Court of Protection for a ruling.

## Organ retention and the Human Tissue Act 2004

In the 1990s, inquiries at the Bristol Royal Infirmary and the Royal Liverpool Children's Hospital, Alder Hey, brought to light the routine practice of removing organs from dead bodies and retaining them indefinitely. In some cases the tissue was used, but in the majority of cases it was simply stored without the consent or even knowledge of relatives. A common theme arising from the evidence given by relatives affected was that they would have been happy to gift organs, had they been asked.

The Human Tissue Act 2004 was enacted as a response to these revelations and was designed to prevent this from occurring again. Although the retention of organs is now, and was previously, legal, the current framework requires consent from the relatives after death or from the deceased themselves before death. Use or storage of organs without appropriate consent has become a criminal offence, punishable by up to 3 years in prison with or without a fine of up to £6000. Similarly tissues, including pathology slides, cannot be retained without consent.

## Post-mortems and death certification

### Death certificates and cremation forms

A death must be registered for there to be a funeral. This means that a death certificate (Box 11.4) must be completed with a cause of death. Death may only be certified by a doctor who attended the deceased during the last illness and seen them within the 14 days before death, or seen the body after death. Certification may be completed by a general practitioner or by a hospital doctor who gives a cause of death to the best of their knowledge ('old age' should not be given as a cause of death unless a more specific cause cannot be given and the patient was at least 70: even in these situations the registrar of deaths may reject the certificate if the patient died in hospital). For the majority of cases this is all that is required. However, if there is no doctor who meets these requirements or no doctor can give a cause of death, the death must be reported to the coroner in England and Wales, and the procurator fiscal in Scotland.

> **Box 11.4 Types of death certificate**
>
> 1 Stillbirth certificate (after 24 weeks of pregnancy)
>
> 2 Neonatal death certificate (any death up to 28 days after birth)
>
> 3 Medical certificate of cause of death (all other deaths) (Figure 11.3).

Cremation forms have two parts that must be completed. The first part should ideally be completed by the doctor who completed the death certificate. The doctor completing this part must have seen the patient before death and the body after death. The term 'ordinary medical attendant' on the form usually refers to the deceased's GP, not the hospital doctor who cared for the patient. The second part should be completed by an independent doctor who was not responsible for caring for the deceased and who has been registered with the General Medical Council for at least 5 years.

### Coroners' post-mortems

There are a number of types of death that must always be reported to a coroner:

- When the deceased was not seen by a doctor during his last illness
- When the cause of death is unknown or uncertain
- Violent, accidental or unnatural deaths (including septicaemia originating from an injury)
- Fall or accident in the previous 12 months
- Death from neglect
- Hypothermia (unless secondary to another condition such as hypothyroidism)

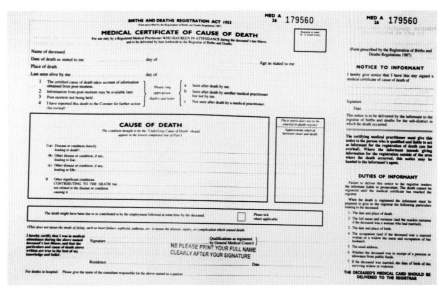

**Figure 11.3** An adult death certificate.

- Sudden or unexpected deaths, including maternal deaths related to pregnancy
- Deaths in suspicious circumstances
- Deaths within 24 hours of hospital admission unless admitted for terminal care
- Deaths related to invasive procedures or surgery (any death within 14 days of surgery should be discussed with the coroner)
- Deaths related to anaesthesia at any time during or after the anaesthetic
- Suicides
- Drug-related (including acute alcohol poisoning, solvent abuse, therapeutic and recreational drugs and blood transfusion) deaths
- Poisoning, including food poisoning
- Industrial illnesses (such as asbestosis) and industrial poisoning (even if not the actual cause of death)
- Methicillin-resistant *Staphylococcus aureus* (MRSA)-related deaths where the MRSA was contracted in hospital as a result of a procedure and contributed to death
- Deaths where the deceased was detained under the Mental Health Act 1983
- Deaths in prison or young offenders' institutions
- Deaths resulting from termination of pregnancy
- Alleged stillbirths when the child may have been born alive
- It is advised that any death thought to be due to medical mismanagement is also reported.

Sometimes it may not be immediately obvious that the death is reportable: for example, death may be due to bronchopneumonia but the underlying cause was a fall leading to a fractured neck of femur and surgical repair and should thus be discussed with the coroner (Box 11.5). Lines and other equipment should not be removed from the body (Box 11.6) once the coroner is notified of a death they may be satisfied that a death certificate can be issued but if not he will order a post-mortem. The pathologist carries this out under the authority of the coroner to try to determine the cause of death. There is no right to object to a coroner's post-mortem, and consent is unnecessary. Under the Human Tissue Act 2004, relatives have the right to decide what happens to tissue removed in a coroner's post-mortem after the examination is completed. If a pathologist wishes to retain tissue taken during a coroner's post-mortem they must obtain appropriate consent as defined in the Act. This means a valid consent from someone in a qualifying relationship with the deceased, as explained earlier.

---

**Box 11.5 Information to have available when reporting a death**

- Name, age and address of the deceased
- Name of GP
- Name of the practitioner who confirmed death
- Place, time and date of death
- Information about current illness or admission (such as operations performed)

---

- Past medical history
- Occupation of the deceased
- Name and contact number of next of kin.

---

**Box 11.6 Removal of lines and other equipment after death**

If the death is reportable to the coroner all equipment attached to the patient should be left in place until the case is discussed with the coroner's officer. However, some equipment (such as ventilators) may be needed for another patient and it is permissible if necessary to remove this equipment.

The following should be left in place:

- Endotracheal tubes
- Drains
- Sutures
- Intravenous lines (central and peripheral)
- Arterial lines
- Nasogastric, nasojejunal and other feeding tubes
- Urinary catheters
- Defibrillation pads
- Pacing devices.

If any equipment is thought to be faulty it must be left untouched, preferably in a locked room until discussed with the coroner's office.

---

The post-mortem may provide sufficient information for the death to be registered. However, it may be followed by an inquest if, for example, the death was violent or unnatural. The coroner's remit is to inquire about the cause of a death. A coroner's inquest is a public hearing in open court, to which witnesses are called to give evidence about the death in question. Healthcare professionals may be called as witnesses (it is compulsory to attend once called) and should be prepared to explain medical terms and procedures, as not only are relatives and other lay people usually present but the coroner may not be medically qualified (the coroner can be a doctor, barrister or solicitor). The family can ask questions and may be legally represented. The purpose of the inquest is not to establish if anyone was at fault or to blame for the deaths. It aims to find out (and record) how, when and where the person died and the particulars needed for registration of the death. Matters of blame or fault can only be pursued in separate civil or criminal proceedings, although occasionally where there are allegations of gross negligence it may be relevant to consider a systems failure. Following the hearing, the coroner may report the facts to an appropriate authority that may have power to prevent similar fatalities in future, but they cannot make recommendations or compel the authority to take action. Where there is a question of criminal proceedings, the inquest may be adjourned until a more suitable time.

## Hospital post-mortems

Hospital post-mortems may be carried out when a coroner's post-mortem has not been ordered. This may be in a situation where the death is not suspicious, but the doctor or relatives want to know more about the cause of death. The post-mortem should be carried out after the death certificate has been issued: the doctor should circle the statement that information from a post-mortem may be available later. Hospital post-mortems are only lawful if there has been appropriate consent, as required by the Human Tissue Act 2004. This means the written consent of the deceased before the death, a nominated representative or a qualifying relative, as explained earlier. In the case of a child parental consent is necessary.

**Case with key points:** *Re Y (Mental Incapacity: Bone Marrow Transplant)* **[1996] 2 FLR 787**

***Background***: Y was a severely mentally and physically handicapped adult who was unable to consent to donate bone marrow to her sister. Receiving Y's bone marrow was the sister's only real chance of recovery: there was no other suitable match.

The family asked the court to approve a bone marrow harvest from Y.

***Court Ruling***: Best interests are not exclusively medical interests. In this case, the bone marrow harvest was of very low risk and Y did not object to the procedure. There was a plausible benefit to Y: Y's close relationship with her mother would be negatively affected by her sister's death.

***Key points***: Emotional and social interests must be included in the balancing act with medical interests when assessing best interests. This case cannot be a precedent for more intrusive procedures, such as solid organ donation, since these carry much higher risks.

## Further reading

Erin CA, Harris J. An ethical market in human organs. *Journal of Medical Ethics* 2003; 29(3): 137–138.

Jackson E. *Medical Law: Text, Cases and Materials.* Oxford University Press, Oxford, 2006.

Wilkinson S. *Bodies for Sale: Ethics and Exploitation in the Human Trade.* Routledge, 2003.

# CHAPTER 12

# The Healthcare Professional and the Human Rights Act

*Ingrid Granne[1] and Lorraine Corfield[2]*

[1] Clinical Research Fellow and Specialist Registrar, Nuffield Department of Obstetrics and Gynaecology, University of Oxford, UK
[2] Senior Vascular Fellow, Guy's and St Thomas' NHS Trust, London, UK

---

**OVERVIEW**

- Human rights, as drawn up by the European Convention on Human Rights, are now part of UK law.

- All laws made by parliament and all legal judgments must be compatible with the Human Rights Act.

- Human Rights may be absolute or limited.

---

Recognition of the inherent dignity and of the equal and inalienable rights of all members of the human family is the foundation of freedom, justice and peace in the world

*– Convention on the Rights of the Child*

The European Convention on Human Rights was drawn up in 1950. It was intended to enshrine fundamental civil and political rights. This binding agreement between countries has meant that since 1966 British citizens have had the right to apply to the European Commission for Human Rights if they felt their rights under the Convention had been breached by the state.

The Convention was formally written into English law as the Human Rights Act 1998 (and into Scottish law as the Scotland Act 1998). The Act is a clear legal statement of the basic rights and fundamental freedoms that individuals can expect from the state. Since the Act came into force, citizens have been able to look to the domestic legal system for redress if their human rights have been breached rather than having to apply directly to the European Commission. It also means that not only do the courts have to consider whether their judgments are consistent with the Human Rights Act, but parliament must also make laws that are consistent with the Act.

The rights described by the Human Rights Act relate to what individuals can expect of public bodies, including the National Health Service. The law demands that all public bodies ensure that everything that they do is compatible with Convention rights. However, the Human Rights Act does not apply to private concerns, such as a private nursing home or private hospital.

## Absolute and limited rights

It is widely accepted that not all rights are absolute. This is because the rights of one individual (such as, the right to express oneself freely) may come into conflict with the rights of another individual (for example, their right to a private life). In addition, the interests of the wider community or the state may also need to be taken into account. Thus the necessity to promote public health may in certain circumstances limit the rights of an individual.

Most of the human rights described by the Act are set out in Articles which have two parts (Box 12.1). The first part of each Article describes the right and the second part describes how and in what circumstance that right may be limited. For example, Article 8 states that everyone has a right to respect for his family and private life. However, the Article goes on to state that the right may be waived under certain circumstances (thus, it is a limited right). These circumstances include the protection of health, the protection of morals or the protection of the rights and freedoms of others. However, if the right is to be limited, the law states that the interference must be necessary in a democratic society. There must be a pressing societal need to limit an individual's rights.

Although most of the human rights protected by the Act are limited, there are some rights that are considered to be so essential that there can be no circumstances in which that right can be contravened. These are described as absolute rights. For example, Article 3 says, 'No one shall be subjected to torture or to inhuman or degrading treatment or punishment.' This right cannot be lawfully breached under any circumstances.

---

Box 12.1 **Relevant Articles in the Human Rights Act**

**Article 2**

Everyone's right to life shall be protected by law. No one shall be deprived of his life intentionally save in the execution of a sentence of a court following conviction in respect of a crime for which this penalty is provided by law.

   Deprivation of life shall not be regarded as inflicted in contravention of this article when it results from the use of force which is no more than absolutely necessary: in defence of any person from unlawful violence; in order to effect a lawful arrest or to prevent escape of a person lawfully detained; in action lawfully taken for the purpose of quelling a riot or insurrection.

---

*ABC of Medical Law.* By Lorraine Corfield, Ingrid Granne
and William Latimer-Sayer. Published 2009 by Blackwell Publishing,
ISBN 978-1-4501-7628-6

**Article 3**

No one shall be subjected to torture or to inhuman or degrading treatment or punishment.

**Article 8**

Everyone has the right to respect for his private and family life, his home and his correspondence.

There shall be no interference by a public authority with the exercise of this right except such as is in accordance with the law and is necessary in a democratic society in the interests of national security, public safety or the economic well-being of the country, for the prevention of disorder or crime, for the protection of health or morals, or for the protection of the rights and freedoms of others.

**Article 9**

Everyone has the right to freedom of thought, conscience and religion; this right includes freedom to change his religion or belief, and freedom, either alone or in community with others and in public or private, to manifest his religion or belief, in worship, teaching, practice and observance. Freedom to manifest one's religion or beliefs shall be subject only to such limitations as are prescribed by law and are necessary in a democratic society in the interests of public safety, for the protection of public order, health or morals, or the protection of the rights and freedoms of others.

**Article 12**

Men and women of marriageable age have the right to marry and to found a family, according to the national laws governing the exercise of this right.

**Article 14**

The enjoyment of the rights and freedoms set forth in the Convention shall be secured without discrimination on any ground such as sex, race, colour, language, religion, political or other opinion, national or social origin, association with a national minority, property, birth or other status.

## The Human Rights Act and medical law

It is becoming increasingly clear that the Human Rights Act is of relevance in many areas of medical law. It is likely that in future the Human Rights Act will be used in many more medico-legal cases. The Articles most likely to be of relevance are reviewed subsequently with some examples of how the courts have evaluated cases. They are by no means exhaustive but demonstrate the application of human rights law to medicine.

## Article 2

### Decisions with regard to life-sustaining treatment
#### Withdrawing artificial hydration and nutrition in cases of permanent vegetative states
The courts have considered whether withdrawing artificial nutrition and hydration from patients in a permanent vegetative state contravened their right to life. In *Airedale NHS Trust v Bland* (2002)

the courts found that there is a legal difference between omitting to feed and hydrate a patient and the act of deliberately killing that patient. The responsibility of the state to safeguard life is not absolute. Article 2 is not breached unless it can be proven that there was an obligation to act to save the patient. In the case of medical care, there is a positive obligation on the state to safeguard life only when it is in a person's best interests or at the person's request.

### The right to die
The courts have considered whether Article 2 also implies a right to die at the time of one's choosing. In *Pretty v United Kingdom* (2002) the European Court found that a terminally ill woman did not have a legal right under the Convention to assisted suicide.

### Abortion
The European courts have looked at Article 2 of the Convention with regard to abortion on several occasions. In a case where a prospective father challenged the right of his ex-partner to obtain termination of pregnancy (*Paton v UK* (1980)), the courts rejected the notion that the foetus has an absolute right to life. In a later case (*Vo v France* (2005)), the court suggested that the foetus deserved to be treated with dignity, but did not go as far as to ascribe the foetus Article 2 rights.

## Article 3
### Cardiopulmonary resuscitation
The Human Rights Act may be of relevance in decisions regarding 'do not resuscitate' orders. Some patients may feel that if cardiopulmonary resuscitation (CPR) were to carry with it the possible prospect of being kept alive in total dependence or with a permanent lack of awareness this would be so awful as to amount to inhuman and degrading treatment. Thus the Article 2 duty to protect life must be weighed against the obligation not to subject an individual to such inhuman or degrading treatment, as well as having regard for the patient's wishes (see Chapter 9).

### Treatment without consent
In *Herczegfalvy v Austria* (1992) a man was compulsorily detained as he was considered to be a danger to others because of his mental illness. He asked the court to rule whether the forcible administration of food and neuroleptics and the use of handcuffs and a security bed to administer treatment constituted inhuman or degrading treatment. The European Court found that in extreme circumstances medical treatment without consent may be considered to be inhuman or degrading treatment. When incompetent patients are treated lawfully in their best interests (under the Mental Capacity Act) Article 3 is not breached. However, if competent patients are treated without their consent and the effect of the treatment is sufficiently serious, Article 3 may be violated. In this particular case, the court found that Article 3 rights had not been breached but commented that in cases of psychiatric care the imbalance of power between doctor and patient means that hospitals must be particularly vigilant to comply with Convention rights.

## Article 8
### The right to physical integrity
Human rights may be interpreted by the courts relatively broadly. In an English case (*Glass v United Kingdom* (2004)) the courts were asked to decide if the actions of a hospital trust breached the Article 8 rights of a child. A boy with severe learning difficulties was admitted with a respiratory tract infection to hospital. The medical staff advised the family that the child was dying. A 'do not resuscitate' order was documented in the notes without his mother's knowledge. A diamorphine infusion was commenced against the wishes of his mother. He deteriorated overnight but resuscitation was not initiated by the medical team. However, his mother successfully resuscitated her son and brought legal action.

As the child lacked capacity, his mother was the legal proxy. The European Court found that the right to private life included the right to physical integrity and the use of the diamorphine infusion without the consent of his mother therefore breached his Article 8 rights. Article 8 was therefore 'engaged' in this case.

This case illustrates that once a court has found that an Article is engaged it must then go on to consider if the right is waived (if it is a limited right). Article 8 is limited and the court considered the three situations in which it could be waived. The court accepted that the medical staff who treated the child acted in accordance with the law; they used the defence of necessity in an emergency. The court also agreed that the interference had a legitimate aim; the doctors considered that the treatment (including withholding CPR) was in the child's best interest. However, the court found that the doctors' interference was not necessary as they should and could have applied for court approval for the treatment they felt should be carried out.

This case confirmed that overriding parents' decision regarding treatment of their child may breach Article 8. It also served to emphasize that a court ruling must be sought if there is disagreement between doctors and parents before the situation becomes urgent. Such rulings can be arranged very quickly in urgent situations and can be obtained out of hours if necessary.

### Confidentiality
Article 8 has been found to be engaged with reference to patient records and confidentiality. In *Z v Finland* (1997), where a crime had been committed by an HIV-positive individual (X) and medical records about his spouse (Z) were taken by police. Doctors were required to testify about her health in an open court revealing her name and her HIV status. The European court found that her Article 8 rights had been engaged and that although the police had a legitimate aim in what they had done, the publication of her identity was not necessary and thus Article 8 had been breached.

## Article 9
### The right to religious freedom
The courts have been asked to judge whether the right to religious freedom allowed a Muslim father to have his son circumcized against the wishes of the child's non-Muslim mother (*Re J* [1999]).

Article 9 is a limited right. In this case the courts decided that the right of a father to choose for his son to be circumcized could be limited if his rights conflicted with the rights or freedoms of the other parent or the child. His right could also be limited if circumcision was not found to be in the best interests of the child. The circumcision was therefore not allowed.

## Article 14
### Protection from discrimination
Article 14 does not give general protection from discrimination to an individual. It works to protect individuals from discrimination in exercising their other convention rights. For example, if a doctor breached the confidentiality of a patient with learning difficulties, assuming that the patient would not be able to give consent, Article 14 as well as Article 8 may be invoked.

---

**Case with key points: *Evans v UK* [2006] 43 EHRR 21**

***Background***: E sought fertility treatment with her partner J prior to having an operation to remove both of her ovaries because of borderline ovarian malignancies. They consented to treatment together in the knowledge that either of them could withdraw their consent at any time. E underwent a cycle of IVF and the resulting eggs were fertilised with J's sperm. The resulting embryos were frozen. After the breakdown of the relationship J wished the embryos to be destroyed. E applied initially to the domestic courts and then to the European Court claiming that this action was in breach of Articles 8 and 14. She also claimed that the embryos were entitled to protection under Articles 2 and 8.

***Court decision***: The court agreed that Article 8 included the decision to have or not to have genetically related children. Thus there was an inevitable conflict between the rights of the two individuals concerned. The court decided that E had no more right to a genetically related child than J had the right to not want that child. This is an example of the court considering the balance of rights of different people. The court also considered the government's view that the wider public interest is not served if patients' consent or withdrawal of consent is not respected. Since the court did not find that the claimant's rights had been violated with regard to Article 8, they did not have to consider whether she had suffered discrimination. The court also found that Article 2 was not applicable to the embryo.

***Key points***: Embryos do not have a right to life within the meaning of Article 2. As Article 8 is a limited right, the right of a person to a private life may be limited by the rights of another. The courts also take into account public interest issues.

---

## Further reading

The Department of Constitutional Affairs. A guide to the human rights act, 1998. http://www.justice.gov.uk/docs/act-studyguide.pdf [2008]

The impact of the Human Rights Act 1998 on medical decision making, 2007. http://www.bma.org.uk/ap.nsf/Content/HumanRightsAct [2008]

# Index

Page numbers in *italics* represent figures, those in **bold** represent tables.